BROOK FARM

GARLAND REFERENCE LIBRARY
OF THE HUMANITIES
(VOL. 122)

BROOK FARM
An Annotated Bibliography and Resources Guide

Joel Myerson

GARLAND PUBLISHING, INC. • NEW YORK & LONDON
1978

© 1978 by Joel Myerson
All rights reserved

Library of Congress Cataloging in Publication Data
Myerson, Joel.
  Brook Farm.
  (Garland reference library of the humanities; v. 122)
  Includes index.
  1. Brook Farm—Bibliography. I. Title.
Z7164.S67M94   016.335'9'74461   78-6382
ISBN 0-8240-9821-8

Printed on acid-free, 250-year-life paper
Manufactured in the United States of America

CONTENTS

Introduction vii

Section A: Members 1
Section B: Visitors 27
Section C: Contemporaries 41
Section D: Histories 49
Section E: The *Harbinger* 69
Section F: Ana 75
Section G: Manuscripts 79

Index 105

INTRODUCTION

Brook Farm: An Annotated Bibliography and Resources Guide is a selective, annotated list of writings about, and a guide to manuscript collections containing information on, the Brook Farm community and its members. It presents and comments upon the important manuscript and printed materials necessary for the study of Brook Farm, including books, reviews of books, contributions in books, articles, M.A. theses, and Ph.D. dissertations. Readers will find it especially strong in listing firsthand accounts of the community, many of which are previously unrecorded. My guiding principle has been to list the truly useful materials in a qualitative, rather than quantitative, manner.

I have personally examined every item in this bibliography, in either the original or a photocopy of the original. In some cases I was unable to locate a copy of the original printing; for these I have supplied what bibliographical information I know and have listed the reprint source I used. In other cases, I worked from clippings; for these, I have supplied whatever bibliographical information is available.

In an author bibliography a chronological arrangement presents an accurate picture of the development of the author's writing or depicts the author's critical reception far better than an alphabetical or topical arrangement. A chronological listing of materials on Brook Farm, however, serves no real purpose other than tracing its early reception in periodicals, and I have therefore arranged this book topically as follows:

Section A: Members lists works by Brook Farmers on the community, and works on Brook Farmers by contemporaries and later writers.

Introduction • viii

Section B: Visitors lists writings on Brook Farm by visitors to the community, and writings on those visitors by others, which comment on their relations with Brook Farm.

Section C: Contemporaries lists writings on Brook Farm by contemporaries without firsthand knowledge of the community.

Section D: Histories lists general accounts of the community by later writers. No systematic attempt has been made to list the many general and uninformative references to Brook Farm in general histories of American literature and culture.

Section E: The *Harbinger* lists studies which deal entirely with the Brook Farm paper. Writings in the *Harbinger* dealing with Brook Farm are listed in Section A.

Section F: Ana lists creative works on Brook Farm and material incorrectly assumed to deal with the community.

Section G: Manuscripts lists the contents of the manuscript collections dealing with Brook Farm at the Boston Public Library, Kansas State Historical Society, Massachusetts Historical Society, Middlebury College Library, and University of Notre Dame Library. These collections are all available for use either through micropublication or through individual photocopy orders.

This book is part of my ongoing study of American Transcendentalism. I would like to thank Carlton Lowenberg for graciously allowing me use of his collection of Brook Farm material. I am grateful to Robert Buckeye, John D. Cushing, Ellen M. Feeney, Walter Harding, William Henry Harrison, Harrison M. Hayford, Carolyn Jakeman, Richard Colles Johnson, James Lawton, and Marcia Moss for their help. I wish to express my appreciation to the following libraries and their staffs for help in using their collections: Boston Athenaeum, Boston Public Library, Concord Free Public Library, Fruitlands Museums Libraries, Harvard University Libraries, Massachusetts Historical Society, The Newberry Library,

Introduction • ix

Northwestern University Library, and University of North Carolina Library. The staff of the University of South Carolina Library has been of great help, especially Beverly Brooks and Claudia Drum.

The University of South Carolina Research and Productive Scholarship Committee has generously provided material assistance in the preparation of this book. I am grateful to the late John R. Welsh and William H. Nolte for their support. I also wish to thank the following student and research assistants: James Ervin, Robert Hungerford, Robert A. Morace, Cameron Northouse, Zenobia Rhue, and especially Robert E. Burkholder.

Joel Myerson
Columbia, South Carolina
1 April 1978

SECTION A: MEMBERS

MEMBERS

ANONYMOUS

A 1   "The Brook Farm Coterie," New York Star, 3 November 1878.

 Interviews with Emerson and Dwight concerning their recollections of Brook Farm and Charles A. Dana. Reprinted in Kenneth Walter Cameron, Transcendental Log (Hartford: Transcendental Books, 1973), pp. 318-319.

A 2   "Brook Farm School," Harbinger, 2 (7 March 1846): 208.

 Brief advertisement for the school.

A 3   [Constitution of the Brook Farm Phalanx], Harbinger, 1 (23 August 1845): 176.

 Discusses how the members of the ruling council are allowed "to fix the compensation for their own services."

A 4   "Recollections of Brook Farm. Mrs. Julia Ward Howe and Others Tell the Twentieth Century Club About the Famous Sociological Experiment," Boston Evening Transcript, 23 February 1899, p. 9.

 Uninformative summary of talks by Howe, John Codman, Abby Morton Diaz (who was in charge of the Brook Farm kindergarten in its early years), G.W. Cooke, and F.B. Sanborn.

A 5   "Speeches of Messrs. Dana and Ripley at the Festival," Phalanx, 1 (20 April 1844): front wrapper verso.

 Prints parts of the speeches given at Fourier's birthday celebration at Brook Farm.

A 6   "To Our Friends," Harbinger, 2 (21 March 1846): 237-238.

 The Brook Farmers give thanks for the offers of help and encouragement that have arrived since announcement of the fire that destroyed the Phalanstery was made. One such favorable letter is printed. More letters of aid and encouragement are printed in "Correspondence," 2 (28 March, 18 April, 2 May 1846): 255, 299-300, 335-336.

A 7   "The West Roxbury Community," <u>New-York Daily Tribune</u>, 13 August 1842, p. 1.

>   Prints an extract from "a private letter from a gentleman who is a member of the Community," expressing his "confidence" about Brook Farm's chances for success.

A 8   "Brook Farm. What it was and What it Aimed to Be," <u>Christian Register</u>, 61 (9 March 1882): 1.

>   Reports an address on Ripley by O.B. Frothingham, and general recollections of Brook Farm life by Dwight and James Sturgis. Recorded by Belle C. Barrows.

ANNA BLACKWELL

A 9   Betham-Edwards, M. "A Survivor of 'Brook Farm,'" <u>The Sketch</u> [England], 23 (24 August 1898): 210.

>   General description of the "daily programme" of the community as related by Anna Blackwell, who was at Brook Farm for "some weeks" in 1842.

GEORGE P. BRADFORD

A 10   Bradford, George P. "Reminiscences of Brook Farm," <u>Century Magazine</u>, 45 (November 1892): 141-148.

>   Bradford joined the community at the beginning, in May 1841. His account is more valuable for his detailed descriptions of daily life at Brook Farm and its social organization than for his brief sketches of the other participants and visitors.

A 11   Ripley, George, and George P. Bradford. "Philosophic Thought in Boston," in <u>The Memorial History of Boston</u>, 4 vols., ed. Justin Winsor, 4:295-330. Boston: James R. Osgood, 1881.

>   Valuable first-hand account of Brook Farm and its members (311-320).

BROOK FARM ASSOCIATION FOR INDUSTRY AND EDUCATION

A 12   Brook Farm Association for Industry and Education. <u>Constitution of the Brook Farm Association for Industry and Education, West Roxbury, Mass. With an Introductory Statement</u>. Boston: I.R. Butts, 1844.

>   Valuable twelve-page statement of Brook Farm's aims and methods.

A 13   Brook Farm Association for Industry and Education. <u>Constitution of the Brook Farm Association for Industry and Education, West Roxbury, Mass. With an Introductory Statement. Second edition, with the By-Laws of the Association.</u> Boston: I.R. Butts, 1844.

    Valuable twenty-page statement about Brook Farm's aims and methods.

BROOK FARM PHALANX

A 14   Brook Farm Phalanx. <u>Constitution of the Brook Farm Phalanx, Adopted May 1, 1845.</u> [Boston: n.p., 1845].

    This valuable fourteen-page statement of goals and methods describes how the community was reorganized "in accordance with the system of Association and the laws of Universal Unity as discovered by CHARLES FOURIER."

JOHN STILLMAN BROWN

A 15   <u>Guide to the Microfilm Edition of the John Stillman Brown Family Papers 1818-1907</u>, ed. Joseph W. Snell. Topeka: Kansas State Historical Society, 1967.

    Reel One ("Correspondence and Papers, 1818-1857") contains a number of letters dealing with Brown's stay at Brook Farm. See also G 33-G 51.

REBECCA CODMAN BUTTERFIELD

A 16   Crawford, Mary Caroline. "Brook Farm: An Essay in Socialism," in her <u>Romantic Days in Old Boston</u>, pp. 24-54. Boston: Little, Brown, 1910.

    General account of the community, drawing upon Crawford's conversations with a former Brook Farmer, Mrs. Rebecca Codman Butterfield; illustrated.

A 17   Cutter, M. Gertrude. "Brook Farm Reminiscences," <u>Good Health</u>, 45 (September 1910): 751-760.

    Valuable interview with Mrs. Rebecca Codman Butterfield, who was at Brook Farm from May 1843 until the end, concerning the daily and social life of the community; illustrated.

A 18   Chubb, Edwin Watts. "Curtis and Hawthorne at the Brook Farm," in his <u>Stories of Authors</u>, pp. 266-269. New York: Sturgis & Walton, 1910.

Sketches for young people, based on Ora Sedgwick's article (A 134); of no value.

JOHN THOMAS CODMAN

A 19   Brook Farm. Historic and Personal Memoirs by Dr. John Thomas Codman. [Boston: Arena, 1894].

Publisher's brochure, quoting from reviews and from letters by S. Willard Saxton and Edwin F. Waters to Codman giving their general recollections of Brook Farm.

A 20   "The Brook Farm Movement," Boston Herald, 4 April 1895.

Brief and uninformative account of a talk on Brook Farm by John Codman.

A 21   Codman, John T. "The Brook Farm Association," Coming Age, 2 (July 1899): 33-38.

General account of the history, daily life, and goals of the community.

A 22   Codman, John Thomas. Brook Farm: Historic and Personal Memoirs. Boston: Arena, 1894.

Codman was twenty-seven when he arrived at Brook Farm with his family in March 1843; he left after the Phalanstery fire in 1846. His account of the origin of the community is dull and derivative, but his description of how Brook Farm was reorganized into a Fourierist phalanx is excellent for its account of how the Brook Farmers put theory into practice. Along with Marianne Dwight's Letters from Brook Farm (A 48), this is probably the best comprehensive account of life at the community by a resident. Readers should be forewarned that Codman is not particular about his chronology and his dating of events, and the placing of them in his story is often confusing. Also included are valuable appendices containing "Students' and Inquirers' Letters," "Applicants' Letters and Mr. Ripley's Replies," Charles Lane's "Brook Farm" (B 59), and "Associative Articles" by Dwight, William Henry Channing, Horace Greeley, Fourier, and Albert Brisbane.

Reviews:

Phillips, Paul. "The History of Brook Farm," Arena, 10 (November 1894): xxii-xxvi. Codman has succeeded in bringing Brook Farm to life.
"The Listener," Boston Evening Transcript, 14 November 1894, p. 4. Codman's book will counteract those accounts which consider Brook Farm a "ridiculous failure."

      Christian Register, 29 November 1894. The book suffers
         from being short on facts and long on anecdotes.
      "Brook Farm Memoirs," Boston Herald, 2 December 1894.
         Codman's is the best account yet of the community,
         though his narrative lacks form and completeness.
      Higginson, T.W. Harvard Graduate's Magazine, 3 (March
         1895): 433-434. Codman's book is "roughly executed"
         and contains numerous errors, which Higginson corrects.
      [Chadwick, John White.] Nation, 60 (14 March 1895):
         207-208. This book "adds little of importance" to our
         knowledge of Brook Farm and "does little credit to the
         author's judgment, taste, or skill."
      "Memories of Brook Farm," Dial, 18 (16 March 1895): 184.
         This is an "extremely interesting" and "instructive"
         book.
      Haynes, George H. Annals of the American Academy, 5
         (May 1895): 967-968. The author speaks with
         "authority and interest."
      Howells, W.D. "Life and Letters," Harper's Weekly
         Magazine, 39 (31 August 1895): 820. Although Codman's
         account of Brook Farm might have been "more solidly
         and weightily" told, it is an interesting and
         informative book. Partially reprinted as "Brook Farm
         and Modern Socialism," Conservator, 6 (September 1895):
         108-109.
      Doucet, J. Homer. "Brook Farm: Historic and Personal
         Memoirs," Conservator, 6 (December 1895): 155-157.
         Codman has rendered a "great service" by telling his
         story of the community.

A 23 Codman, John Thomas. "The Men and Thought that Made the
      Boston of the Forties Famous," Coming Age, 2 (September
      1899): 239-247.

      An interview with Codman about the members and goals of
      Brook Farm.

A 24 Bemis, Edward W. "Coöperation in New England," Johns Hopkins
      University Studies in Historical and Political Science,
      6th series (1888): 15-133.

      Prints a brief letter from John Codman to the author
      about Brook Farm, concluding: "Brook Farm life and
      theories made me believe that industrial, and with it
      social progress, is the foundation of society and of our
      nation" (18).

GEORGE WILLIAM CURTIS

A 25 Early Letters of George Wm. Curtis to John S. Dwight: Brook
      Farm and Concord, ed. George Willis Cooke. New York:
      Harpers, 1898.

Cooke prints forty-one letters written from Curtis to
Dwight from New York, Concord, and Italy between August
1843 and April 1847, twenty-one letters written between
October 1850 and May 1886, and his own introduction on
Brook Farm, drawn mainly from other published accounts.
The title is misleading for, though Curtis was at Brook
Farm from the spring of 1842 until October 1843, all the
letters were written after he had left the community,
and touch on Brook Farm itself only briefly. More
interesting are Curtis' comments on the Brook Farmers he
meets, such as Christopher Pearse Cranch, William Henry
Channing, Isaac Hecker, and Charles A. Dana, in New York,
and Emerson and Hawthorne in Concord.

Reviews:

"Books of the Day," <u>Boston Evening Transcript</u>, 31 August
1898, p. 10. The publication of Curtis' letters
should help renew interest in Brook Farm.
<u>Nation</u>, 67 (15 September 1898): 209-210. These letters
are "a fine disclosure of the working of Transcendentalism in a singularly ardent and ingenuous youth."

A 26 [Curtis, George William.] "Editor's Easy Chair," <u>Harper's
New Monthly Magazine</u>, 38 (January 1869): 268-271.

General discussion of Hawthorne and his appearance at
Brook Farm. Reprinted as "Hawthorne and Brook Farm,"
in Curtis' <u>From the Easy Chair. Third Series</u> (New York:
Harpers, 1894), pp. 1-19.

A 27 [Curtis, George William.] "Editor's Easy Chair," <u>Harper's
New Monthly Magazine</u>, 40 (February 1870): 455-457.

A description of the Brook Farm delegation's appearance
at a Boston concert.

A 28 [Curtis, George William.] "Editor's Easy Chair," <u>Harper's
New Monthly Magazine</u>, 53 (August 1876): 464-466.

General comments on the intellectual atmosphere of New
England at the time Brook Farm was started.

A 29 [Curtis, George William.] "Editor's Easy Chair," <u>Harper's
New Monthly Magazine</u>, 63 (November 1881): 947-948.

Describes the Brook Farmers' attendance at musical events
in Boston.

A 30 Cary, Edward. <u>George William Curtis</u>. Boston: Houghton,
Mifflin, 1894.

Information on Curtis and his brother Burrill at Brook
Farm, drawn from unpublished manuscripts (pp. 19-31).

A 31 Cooke, George Willis. "George William Curtis at Concord," *Harper's New Monthly Magazine*, 96 (December 1897): 137-149.

>   Letters from Curtis to Dwight from 3 March 1844 to 25 October 1845. Reprinted in *Early Letters of George Wm. Curtis to John S. Dwight*, ed. Cooke (A 25).

A 32 Lennon, Florence Becker. "The Influence of Brook Farm on George William Curtis 1842-1872." M.A. thesis, University of Colorado, 1947. 94 pp.

>   General account of Curtis at Brook Farm and a survey of his subsequent comments on the community.

A 33 Madden, Edward H. "G.W. Curtis: Practical Transcendentalist," *Personalist*, 40 (Autumn 1959): 369-379.

>   Curtis' Transcendentalism was "more activist and socially oriented" in the Ripley-Parker tradition, making it the guiding principle of his daily life, and not merely "answers to speculative questions."

A 34 Milne, Gordon. *George William Curtis & the Genteel Tradition*. Bloomington: Indiana University Press, 1956.

>   Valuable account of Curtis' residence at Brook Farm. From his stay he gained a strong belief in the "idealistic philosophy," an "Emersonian-like faith in the importance of the individual," and a "moral enthusiasm" that stayed with him throughout his life (pp. 10-19).

CHARLES A. DANA

A 35 [Dana, Charles A.] [Address], *Phalanx*, 1 (20 April 1844): 113-115.

>   Prints Dana's address to the "Grand Convention of the Friends of Association in the United States," one "illustrative of the experience at Brookfarm."

A 36 Dana, Charles A. *A Lecture on Association, in its Connection with Religion*. Boston: Benjamin H. Greene, 1844.

>   Valuable statement of the religious basis of Fourierism.

A 37 Dana, Charles A. "Letter from Charles A. Dana," *Phalanx*, 1 (24 August 1844): 255-257.

>   Prints Dana's letter of 17 June 1844 from Brook Farm describing the success of Fourierism at the community.

A 38   Wilson, James Harrison. *The Life of Charles A. Dana*. New
       York: Harpers, 1907.

       Valuable account of Dana's life at Brook Farm, drawn from
       previously unpublished manuscripts, and summary of Dana's
       later views on the community (pp. 25-60), including the
       printing of his address on Brook Farm at the University
       of Michigan, 21 January 1895 (pp. 517-534).

A 39   Whittier, John Greenleaf. *Whittier Correspondence from the
       Oak Knoll Collections 1830-1892*, ed. John Albree. Salem:
       Essex Book and Print Club, 1911.

       Prints Dana's letter of 3 July 1845 saying he is glad
       Whittier likes the *Harbinger*, and gives his own feelings
       about Brook Farm (pp. 94-95).

J. HOMER DOUCET

A 40   Doucet, J. Homer. "Reminiscences of the Brook Farm
       Association," *Conservator*, 5 (January, February 1895):
       164-165, 180-182; 6 (March 1895): 4-6.

       Doucet was twenty-two when he joined Brook Farm in the
       spring of 1844. He stayed until the summer of 1846.
       His reminiscences are general and recall daily life at
       the community. Brief character sketches of Charles A.
       Dana and Sophia Ripley are included.

JOHN SULLIVAN DWIGHT

A 41   [Dwight, John Sullivan.] "How Stands the Cause?" *Harbinger*,
       3 (7 November 1846): 348-351.

       Brook Farm is not a failure because it is financially
       unsound; rather, it is "the intellectual and moral centre
       of the [Association] movement."

A 42   Dwight, John S. *A Lecture on Association, in its Connection
       with Education*. Boston: Benjamin H. Greene, 1844.

       Valuable statement of the educational basis of Fourierism.

A 43   Dwight, John S. "Music a Means of Culture," *Atlantic
       Monthly*, 26 (September 1870): 321-331.

       The Brook Farm community was a perfect example of the
       worth of music to people as a means of culture.

A 44   Cooke, George Willis. "Brook Farm," in his *John Sullivan
       Dwight: Brook-Farmer, Editor, and Critic of Music*, pp.
       48-128. Boston: Small, Maynard, 1898.

Important account of Dwight's life at the community, drawing upon manuscript sources.

A 45 Fertig, Walter L. "Brook Farm in the Early Years: 1841-1845" and "Association and the Harbinger: 1845-1847," in his "John Sullivan Dwight: Transcendentalist and Literary Amateur of Music," pp. 70-103, 104-174. Ph.D. dissertation, University of Maryland, 1952.

The best biographical study of Dwight and his stay at Brook Farm, using many manuscript sources.

A 46 Shuman, R. Baird. "Dwight Writes Lowell from Brook Farm," Emerson Society Quarterly, No. 27 (II Quarter 1962): 24-25.

Prints Dwight's letter of 13 August 1845 about James Russell Lowell's poetry; nothing on Brook Farm.

A 47 Thomas, J. Wesley. "John Sullivan Dwight: A Translator of German Romanticism," American Literature, 21 (January 1950): 427-441.

Discusses Dwight's work on German authors while at Brook Farm (437-438).

MARIANNE DWIGHT

A 48 Dwight, Marianne. Letters from Brook Farm 1844-1847, ed. Amy L. Reed. Poughkeepsie, N.Y.: Vassar College, 1928.

This is the best book for obtaining a vivid and accurate picture of daily life at Brook Farm, being the only extended discussion of the community told in contemporary documents, rather than in later reminiscences. Marianne Dwight, sister of John Sullivan Dwight, came to Brook Farm in the fall of 1843 at the age of twenty-seven, and stayed until the end. The eighty-four letters here printed (most manuscripts are at the Massachusetts Historical Society; see G 52-G 200) cover from the spring of 1844 to March 1847, and were written to her brother, Frank, and her friend, Anna Q.T. Parsons. They are newsletters and provide an excellent description of the Ripleys, John Orvis (whom Marianne Dwight married at Brook Farm), Dwight, Charles King Newcomb, Albert Brisbane, William Henry Channing, and Charles A. Dana. All the letters are well-annotated. An essential book. Illustrated.

Reviews:

"Letters of a Brook Farm Colonist," New York Times Book Review, 26 August 1928, p. 5. This book "re-creates

the experiment anew" and will be invaluable to all
future studies of the community.

Brooks, Van Wyck. "A Picture of Brook Farm," Independent, 121 (1 September 1928): 212. This book joins Swift's Brook Farm as the most interesting and important study of the community.

Times Literary Supplement, 4 October 1928, p. 714. This book details the daily life in "a very delightful diversion in America of the forties."

KATE SLOAN GASKILL

A 49 "The Last Remaining Brook Farmer (But One)" [Kate Sloan Gaskill]. "A Girl's Recollections of the Brook Farm School," Overland Monthly, 72 (September 1918): 233-240.

Mrs. Gaskill, who was at Brook Farm from June 1843 until the end, recalls the school and its teachers in this general reminiscence.

NATHANIEL HAWTHORNE

A 50 Hawthorne, Nathaniel. The American Notebooks, ed. Randall Stewart. New Haven: Yale University Press, 1932.

Essential first-hand account of Hawthorne's life at Brook Farm from 12 April to late October 1841 (pp. 75-90, 292-295).

A 51 Hawthorne, Nathaniel. The American Notebooks, ed. Claude M. Simpson. Columbus: Ohio State University Press, 1972.

Supersedes the text of Stewart's edition but the latter's notes are still valuable (pp. 196-222, 604-607).

A 52 Hawthorne, Nathaniel. The Blithedale Romance. Boston: Ticknor, Reed, and Fields, 1852.

This fictionalized account of a community with many similarities to Brook Farm and the people there has long been considered Hawthorne's roman à clef about his Brook Farm days. While there is considerable evidence that Hawthorne did partially base his account upon incidents and people at Brook Farm, it would be unwise to read his novel as pure autobiography or to see his characters as having exact counterparts in the real people in the community. A new edition of The Blithedale Romance, edited from Hawthorne's manuscript, was published in 1964 by the Ohio State University Press.

A 53 Hawthorne, Nathaniel. "The Hall of Fantasy," Pioneer, 1 (February 1843): 49-55.

"In the midst of these lights of the age, it gladdened me to meet my old friends of Brook Farm, with whom, though a recreant now, I had borne the heat of many a summer's day, while we labored together towards the perfect life. They seemed so far advanced, however, in the realization of their idea, that their sunburnt faces and toil-hardened frames may soon be denied admittance into the Hall of Fantasy" (52). This passage was deleted by Hawthorne from subsequent printings.

A 54 Love Letters of Nathaniel Hawthorne. 2 vols. Chicago: Society of the Dofobs, 1907.

Important book for the study of Brook Farm, printing most of Hawthorne's letters to Sophia Peabody from there (2:3-33).

A 55 Abel, Darrel. "Hawthorne's Skepticism About Social Reform with Especial Reference to The Blithedale Romance," University of Kansas City Review, 19 (Spring 1953): 181-193.

Hawthorne's skepticism was based on his belief in these errors of the socialist reformers: they had an excessive reliance on merely changing the external patterns of society; they had impractical theories about the possibilities of human association; they had exaggerated notions about human wisdom; and they had a destructive irreverence for the past.

A 56 Anderson, Judith Müller. "Hawthorne's Use of Experience in The Blithedale Romance." M.A. thesis, Texas A & M University, 1967. 132 pp.

Hawthorne used real people and incidents from Brook Farm according to his definition of a "romance," wherein the artist is allowed great latitude in historical accuracy.

A 57 Beatty, Lillian. "Typee and Blithedale: Rejected Ideal Communities," Personalist, 37 (Autumn 1956): 367-378.

Both Melville and Hawthorne rejected their idealized communities because they believed that man should not isolate himself from society, that it is folly to attempt to reform an evil world, and that intellect should not be glorified at the expense of the heart.

A 58 Bell, George H. "Nathaniel Hawthorne, Brook Farm, and The Blithedale Romance." M.A. thesis, University of Oregon, 1957. 117 pp.

General discussion of Hawthorne's stay at the community and his use of it in fiction.

A 59 Böhmer, Lina. Brookfarm und Hawthornes "Blithedale Romance".
        Jena: Universitäts-Buchdruckerei Gustav Neuenhahn, 1936.
        [German]

        This published doctoral dissertation gives a general
        account of the Brook Farm and Blithedale communities, and
        discusses Hawthorne's possible use of his experience and
        friends at Brook Farm in his novel.

A 60 Bounds, Harrison. "Brook Farm and Hawthorne's The Blithedale
        Romance." M.A. thesis, Columbia University, 1949. 62 pp.

        General account of the relationship between the Blithedale
        and Brook Farm communities.

A 61 Bridge, Horatio. Personal Recollections of Nathaniel
        Hawthorne. New York: Harpers, 1893.

        Describes a visit with Hawthorne at Brook Farm (pp.
        84-85).

A 62 Cantwell, Robert. Nathaniel Hawthorne: The American Years.
        New York: Rinehart, 1948.

        General discussion of Hawthorne's stay at Brook Farm
        (pp. 315-333).

A 63 Clarke, Helen Archibald. "The Roxbury Utopia," in her
        Hawthorne's Country, pp. 201-236. Garden City, N.Y.:
        Doubleday, Page, 1913.

        General description of Brook Farm, drawn mainly from
        The Blithedale Romance; illustrated.

A 64 Conway, M.D. "Concerning Hawthorne and Brook Farm," Every
        Saturday Journal, 7 (2 January 1869): 13-18.

        General comments about Hawthorne and the community.
        Reprinted in Kenneth Walter Cameron, Transcendental Log
        (Hartford: Transcendental Books, 1973), pp. 211-215.

A 65 Conway, Moncure D. Life of Nathaniel Hawthorne. London:
        Walter Scott, 1890.

        Brief account of Hawthorne and Brook Farm, drawing upon
        comments made to Conway by Hawthorne's contemporaries,
        and upon Conway's own visit to West Roxbury some years
        after the community disbanded (pp. 84-90).

A 66 Cromphout, Gustaaf Van. "Emerson, Hawthorne, and The
        Blithedale Romance," Georgia Review, 25 (Winter 1971):
        471-480.

An examination of Hawthorne's novel shows that Emerson's ideas on reform are closer to Hawthorne's than is usually supposed.

A 67 Curtis, Alice Cabell. "Hawthorne—His Relations to the Transcendental Movement." M.A. thesis, Cornell University, 1931.

Unimportant account of Hawthorne at Brook Farm (pp. 14-30).

A 68 Curtis, Edith Roelker. "Mr. Hawthorne Arrives in an April Snowstorm," New England Galaxy, 2 (Winter 1961): 17-25.

Reprinted from her A Season in Utopia (D 26).

A 69 Gordon, Joseph T. "Nathaniel Hawthorne and Brook Farm," Emerson Society Quarterly, No. 33 (IV Quarter 1963): 51-61.

Hawthorne's letters and journals show his relations with the community to be "more practical than idealistic." Accordingly, The Blithedale Romance must be taken as it was meant to be—as fiction and not autobiography.

A 70 Hawthorne, Julian. Nathaniel Hawthorne and His Wife. 2 vols. Boston: Houghton, Mifflin, 1884.

Prints valuable letters between Hawthorne, Sophia Peabody, and the Hawthorne family during the Brook Farm period (1:227-237).

A 71 Hawthorne, Julian. "Scenes of Hawthorne's Romances," Century Magazine, 28 (July 1884): 380-397.

Descriptions of Brook Farm in Nathaniel Hawthorne's day and at the time of Julian's writing; illustrated (395-397).

A 72 Hawthorne, Manning. "Hawthorne and Utopian Socialism," New England Quarterly, 12 (December 1939): 726-730.

Prints Hawthorne's letter of 18 July 1841 to David Mack expressing his dissatisfaction with Brook Farm.

A 73 James, Henry. Hawthorne. London: Macmillan, 1879.

Even-handed but skeptical account of the community (pp. 74-90).

A 74 Lang, Hans-Joachim. "The Blithedale Romance: A History of Ideas Approach," in Literatur und Sprache der Vereinigten Staaten: Aufsätze zu Ehren von Hans Galinsky, ed. Hans Helmcke, Klaus Lubbers, and Renate Schmidt-v. Bardeleben, pp. 88-106. Heidelberg: Carl Winter, 1969.

A "more intimate knowledge of Brook Farm, especially in its later, Fourieristic phase," which Hawthorne had "contempt" for, is helpful in seeing how The Blithedale Romance works.

A 75 Lathrop, George Parsons. "At Boston and Brook Farm," in his A Study of Hawthorne, pp. 181-198. Boston: Houghton, Mifflin, 1876.

Early study of Hawthorne's relationship with Brook Farm by his son-in-law.

A 76 McElderry, B.R., Jr. "The Transcendental Hawthorne," Midwest Quarterly, 2 (July 1961): 307-323.

A strain of Transcendentalism can be seen in Hawthorne's thought as expressed in his relations with Brook Farm, in his courtship and marriage, and in his association with Emerson.

A 77 Metzdorf, Robert F. "Hawthorne's Suit Against Ripley and Dana," American Literature, 12 (May 1940): 235-241.

Prints Hawthorne's letter of 6 September 1845 to George Hillard instructing him to bring suit against Ripley or Brook Farm to recover a loan for $524.05 he had made in 1842, and summarizes the results of the subsequent court action in 1846.

A 78 Morris, Lloyd. "A Modern Arcadia," in his The Rebellious Puritan: Portrait of Mr. Hawthorne, pp. 117-150. New York: Harcourt, Brace, 1927.

General account of Hawthorne's stay at Brook Farm and his comments on the community.

A 79 Pritchett, V.S. "Books in General," New Statesman and Nation, 28 (11 November 1944): 323.

Brief account of Hawthorne at Brook Farm.

A 80 Ross, Charles Emmett. "Nathaniel Hawthorne and Brook Farm." M.A. thesis, University of Pittsburgh, 1932. 70 pp.

An examination of Hawthorne's stay at Brook Farm shows that he left disappointed and with "a deepened feeling against Transcendentalism and ill-guided reform."

A 81 Thurman, Kelly. "Margaret Fuller in Two American Novels: The Blithedale Romance and Elsie Venner." M.A. thesis, University of Kentucky, 1945.

Discusses the circumstances behind Hawthorne's use of Fuller as a "prototype" for Zenobia (pp. 1-46).

A 82 Turner, Arlin. "Autobiographical Elements in Hawthorne's
       The Blithedale Romance," University of Texas Studies in
       English, No. 15 (8 July 1935): 39-62.

       The first major study of Hawthorne's use of Brook Farm
       and its members in The Blithedale Romance includes a
       valuable summary of previous comments, especially
       nineteenth-century ones, on the subject. Hawthorne
       "clearly" began planning The Blithedale Romance with
       Brook Farm in mind: numerous parallels between people at
       the community and characters in the novel, between the
       physical setting of Brook Farm and the location of
       Blithedale, between Hawthorne's unsympathetic views of
       reform and Coverdale's, between Hawthorne's experiences
       at Brook Farm and incidents in the novel, and between
       events in Hawthorne's life before and after his stay at
       Brook Farm bear this out. Similar passages in Hawthorne's
       notebooks and letters and in The Blithedale Romance are
       compared in detail.

A 83 Turner, Arlin. "Hawthorne and Reform," New England
       Quarterly, 15 (December 1942): 700-714.

       One reason for Hawthorne's rejection of the ideas behind
       Brook Farm, especially in its later years, was his belief
       that "man's efforts to improve society will continue to
       accomplish nothing until the heart is purified."

A 84 Turrell, Carolyn. "Nathaniel Hawthorne and Brook Farm."
       M.A. thesis, Ohio State University, 1946. 61 pp.

       General account of Hawthorne's relationship with the
       community.

A 85 Ward, William Smith. "Nathaniel Hawthorne and the Brook
       Farm," Letters, 4 (August 1931): 6-14.

       General, uninformative dicussion of Hawthorne at the
       community and his use of it in The Blithedale Romance.

ISAAC T. HECKER

A 86 Hecker, I.T. "Brook Farm," in his Questions of the Soul,
       pp. 59-72. New York: Catholic Publication House, 1855.

       General description of Brook Farm, based largely on the
       accounts of others, though Hecker was himself a member
       from January to July 1843.

A 87 Burton, Katherine. Celestial Homespun: The Life of Isaac
       Thomas Hecker. New York: Longmans, Green, 1943.

       Imaginative reconstruction of Hecker's stay at Brook
       Farm (pp. 35-65).

A 88   Elliott, Walter. <u>The Life of Father Hecker</u>. New York: Columbus Press, 1891.

    Valuable description of Hecker's inward and outward life at Brook Farm, using manuscript sources, including Hecker's diaries and correspondence, and a letter from George William Curtis of 28 February 1890 on Hecker and the community (pp. 42-75).

A 89   Holden, Vincent F. <u>The Early Years of Isaac Thomas Hecker (1819-1844)</u>. Washington: Catholic University of America Press, 1939.

    Valuable study of Hecker's stay at Brook Farm, drawing upon previously unpublished manuscripts (pp. 91-150).

A 90   Holden, Vincent F. <u>The Yankee Paul: Isaac Thomas Hecker</u>. Milwaukee: Bruce, 1958.

    Valuable discussion of Hecker's relationship with Brook Farm, drawing upon manuscript material (pp. 33-55).

GEORGIANA BRUCE KIRBY

A 91   [Kirby, Georgiana Bruce.] "Before I Went to Brook Farm," <u>Old and New</u>, 3 (February 1871): 175-185.

    General account of the circumstances leading up to Kirby's arrival at the community.

A 92   [Kirby, Georgiana Bruce.] "My First Visit to Brook Farm," <u>Overland Monthly</u>, 5 (July 1870): 9-19.

    Kirby lived at Brook Farm from September 1841 to April 1844, while in her mid-twenties, and her accounts of the community are valuable for their portraits of daily life. This article contains information on Charles King Newcomb.

A 93   [Kirby, Georgiana Bruce.] "Reminiscences of Brook Farm," <u>Old and New</u>, 3 (April 1871): 425-438.

    Contains information on Charles A. Dana, Charles King Newcomb, Fuller, Parker, Charles Lane, and Bronson Alcott.

A 94   [Kirby, Georgiana Bruce.] "Reminiscences of Brook Farm," <u>Old and New</u>, 4 (September 1871): 347-358.

    Contains information on Ripley, Dwight, and Brownson.

A 95   [Kirby, Georgiana Bruce.] "Reminiscences of Brook Farm," <u>Old and New</u>, 5 (May 1872): 517-530.

    Contains information on Christopher Pearse Cranch and Fuller.

A 96   Kirby, Georgiana Bruce. Years of Experience: An
        Autobiographical Narrative. New York: Putnams, 1887.

        Valuable reminiscences of Brook Farm, reprinting in part
        her articles in the Overland Monthly and Old and New,
        with additional material (pp. 89-189).

A 97   Myerson, Joel. "Two Unpublished Reminiscences of Brook
        Farm," New England Quarterly, 48 (June 1975): 253-260.

        Prints accounts by Frederick Pratt, detailing the daily
        life at the community during its first four years, and by
        Nora Schelter Blair, describing life at the school during
        the final year of Brook Farm.

CHARLES KING NEWCOMB

A 98   The Journals of Charles King Newcomb, ed. Judith Kennedy
        Johnson. Providence: Brown University Press, 1946.

        Newcomb's residence at Brook Farm from May 1841 to
        December 1845 is discussed, using unpublished manuscript
        sources, in Johnson's introduction (pp. 17-30). The
        journals themselves do not touch on the community.

JOHN ORVIS

A 99   S., W.G.H. "He Was a Brook-Farmer. The Late John Orvis and
        His Work on Social Problems," Boston Evening Transcript,
        20 May 1897, p. 6.

        Biographical account of Orvis, who was at Brook Farm from
        late 1843 until the end, and his connection with the
        community.

FRANCES OSTINELLI

A 100   "The Songstress of Brook Farm," More Books, 12 (March 1937):
        119-120.

        Prints a letter of March 1877 to Dwight about a former
        Brook Farmer, Frances Ostinelli.

GEORGE RIPLEY

A 101   R[ipley]., G[eorge]. "The Angels of the Past," Christian
        Examiner, 42 (May 1847): 343-344.

        This poem is probably Ripley's reflections on the failure
        of Brook Farm.

A 102 [Ripley, George.] "Brook Farm Lecturers," Harbinger, 2 (21 February 1846): 175.

    Describes the lecture tours by John Allen and John Orvis through Massachusetts, Vermont, and New Hampshire on behalf of "the doctrine of Associationism."

A 103 Ripley, George. "Brook Farm School," New-York Weekly Tribune, 25 April 1846, p. 1.

    Description of the community's school.

A 104 [Ripley, George.] "Fire at Brook Farm," Harbinger, 2 (14 March 1846): 220-222.

    Description of the fire at the Phalanstery.

A 105 "People we Meet up and Down the Plaza," New York Leader, ca. early November 1860.

    General account of Ripley's life and his work at Brook Farm. Reprinted in New York Evening Post, 7 November 1860, p. 4; in Littell's Living Age, 67 (1 December 1860): 571-573; in Kenneth Walter Cameron, "Literary News in American Renaissance Newspapers (2)," American Transcendental Quarterly, No. 5 (I Quarter 1970): 69-70; and in Kenneth Walter Cameron, Transcendental Log (Hartford: Transcendental Books, 1973), pp. 145-146.

A 106 "Rev. George Ripley," Monthly Miscellany of Religion and Letters, 4 (May 1841): 293-295.

    It is with "sincere regret" that Ripley's resignation from the ministry is noted. His future plans are not "chimerical or 'Transcendental'" as others have complained, but "both practical and practicable."

A 107 Crowe, Charles R. "The Genesis of a Reformer as Seen in The Letters of George Ripley," Manuscripts, 11 (Spring 1959): 11-13, 38.

    This general discussion of Ripley's change from "a shy young conservative into a socialist reformer" contains little of use.

A 108 Crowe, Charles. George Ripley: Transcendentalist and Utopian Socialist. Athens: University of Georgia Press, 1967.

    The best biography of Ripley, and one of the best documented studies of the Transcendental period, this book contains a valuable presentation of the circumstances and ideas behind Brook Farm.

A 109   [Curtis, George William.] "Editor's Easy Chair," Harper's New Monthly Magazine, 62 (December 1880): 147-148.

Prints an undated letter from Ripley, written from Brook Farm, "valuable as an authoritative exposition of the principle of Brook Farm."

A 110   Duffy, John J. "Transcendental Letters from George Ripley to James Marsh," Emerson Society Quarterly, No. 50 (I Quarter 1968): Supplement 20-24.

Prints Ripley's letter of 17 October 1840 about his plans for Brook Farm. The letter is also printed in Duffy's edition of Marsh's correspondence (C 18).

A 111   Edwards, Channing [Arthur Kinoy]. "'Arise and Depart, For This is not Your Rest': A study of the resignation of George Ripley from the ministry of the Unitarian Church on Purchase Street, in Boston, in the year 1841." Bowdoin Prize Essay, Harvard University, 1941.

Excellent brief (35 pp.) discussion of Ripley's intellectual state immediately before the founding of Brook Farm.

A 112   Frothingham, Octavius Brooks. George Ripley. Boston: Houghton, Mifflin, 1882.

Although outdated, this important first biography of Ripley uses much material now lost, and is therefore still valuable.

A 113   Frothingham, Octavius Brooks. Recollections and Impressions 1822-1890. New York: Putnams, 1891.

Interesting personal appraisal of Ripley and Brook Farm by his friend and biographer (pp. 235-247).

A 114   Howe, Leonard, & Co. Catalogue of a Select Private Library, Containing about 1,000 Volumes, of Very Valuable Theological, Philosophical, and Miscellaneous Books: In the English, French, and German Languages. To Be Sold at Public Auction . . . November 5th, 1846. Boston: Alfred Mudge, 1846.

This is the sale catalogue of Ripley's personal library (and also the bulk of the Brook Farm library) which he sold in partial payment for his debts incurred on the community's behalf. Reprinted in Kenneth Walter Cameron, The Transcendentalists and Minerva, 3 vols. (Hartford: Transcendental Books, 1958), 3:808-817.

A 115   Gohdes, Clarence. "Getting Ready for Brook Farm," Modern
        Language Notes, 49 (January 1934): 36-39.

        Extracts from Ripley's manuscript commonplace book (at
        Harvard University) kept from 1822 to 1840 show that his
        plans for Brook Farm were not based on "quixotic
        idealism," but were a combination of "an intellectual
        ideality with a typical admixture of facts and figures."

A 116   Isely, Jeter A., and Lisette R[iggs]. Isely. "A Note on
        George Ripley and the Beginnings of New England
        Transcendentalism," Proceedings of the Unitarian
        Historical Society, 13 (1961): 75-85.

        General background essay defining Ripley's role in the
        shaping of Transcendentalism up to 1836.

A 117   James, Myrle. "Brook Farm and George Ripley," in her
        "Contributions of the Transcendental Group to the
        Educational Theory in the United States," pp. 16-25.
        M.A. thesis, University of Washington, 1934.

        Brook Farm was the most important example of Transcen-
        dental educational ideas in action.

A 118   Legasse, Viola May. "George Ripley," in her "Transcendental
        Utopianism in America," pp. 26-47. M.A. thesis,
        University of Washington, 1932.

        General, uninformative comments on Brook Farm.

A 119   Riggs, Lisette. "George and Sophia Ripley." Ph.D.
        dissertation, University of Maryland, 1942. 257 pp.

        Valuable account of the founders of Brook Farm, based
        upon many unpublished manuscript sources.

A 120   Schultz, Arthur R., and Henry A. Pochmann. "George Ripley:
        Unitarian, Transcendentalist, or Infidel?" American
        Literature, 14 (March 1942): 1-19.

        Valuable account of the German influences on Ripley's
        thought, especially in the years leading up to and
        including Brook Farm, concluding that he cannot be
        considered an Andrews Norton conservative Unitarian,
        a Parker Transcendentalist, or an infidel. He is a
        perfect example of those idealists who sought to find in
        German philosophy "the means to square their heart by
        their head—to make their religion philosophical, and
        their philosophy religious."

A 121   Wilson, Howard Aaron. "Interlude: Brook Farm, 1841–1845"
          and "George Ripley: Social Critic," in his "George
          Ripley: Social Critic," pp. 68–82, 83–117. Ph.D.
          dissertation, University of Wisconsin, 1941.

          Ripley's social criticism in the Harbinger shows his
          attempts to "make possible the realization of those ideals
          of Christianity and of eighteenth century democracy in
          nineteenth century industrial America." The history of
          Brook Farm is uninformative.

SOPHIA RIPLEY

A 122   Burton, Katherine. "Sophia Dana Ripley," in her In No
          Strange Land: Some American Catholic Converts, pp. 31–42.
          New York: Longmans, Green, 1942.

          General account of Mrs. Ripley's life.

A 123   Burton, Katherine. "Sophia Dana Ripley," Missionary, 53
          (February 1939): 40–43.

          General account of Mrs. Ripley's life, stressing the
          events leading up to her conversion to Catholicism.

A 124   Coleman, Caryl. "A Forgotten Convert," Catholic World, 122
          (November 1925): 192–203.

          General biographical sketch of Mrs. Ripley, stressing
          her conversion to Catholicism.

A 125   Driscoll, Annette S. "A Brook Farm Convert," Ave Maria,
          n.s. 31 (7 June 1930): 705–711.

          General account of Mrs. Ripley, drawing on stories told
          Driscoll by surviving members of the Dana family,
          stressing her conversion to Catholicism.

A 126   Raymond, Henrietta Dana. "Sophia Willard Dana Ripley:
          Co-Founder of Brook Farm." M.A. thesis, Columbia
          University, 1949. 112 pp.

          The best biography of Mrs. Ripley, this study is drawn
          from many unpublished manuscript sources and from
          interviews with family descendants.

AMELIA RUSSELL

A 127   [Russell, Amelia E.] "Home Life of the Brook Farm
          Association," Atlantic Monthly, 42 (October, November
          1878): 458–466, 556–563.

          When Russell joined Brook Farm in about 1843, she was in
          her forties and her perspective is more mature than in

most published reminiscences. Her articles aim to present the "interior life" of the community, both "material and mental." The first part contains information on the Ripleys and Fuller, the second on Horace Greeley.

A 128 Russell, Amelia E. Home Life of the Brook Farm Association. Boston: Little, Brown, 1900.

Revised and expanded version of her Atlantic Monthly articles, with a brief biographical sketch of Russell.

ANNIE SALISBURY

A 129 Salisbury, Annie M. Brook Farm. Marlboro, Mass.: F.B. Estabrook, 1898.

Salisbury was a pupil in the Brook Farm school during 1843. Her brief account is useful only for her recollections of daily life at Brook Farm. Reprinted from the Boston Evening Transcript.

A 130 Salisbury, Annie M. "The Real Brook Farm," Boston Evening Transcript, 27 October, 3 November 1894, pp. 13, 13.

Reprinted as Brook Farm (A 129).

S. WILLARD SAXTON

A 131 Saxton, S. Willard. "A Few Reminiscences of Brook Farm," Pocumtuck Valley Memorial Association Proceedings, 6 (1921): 371-386.

Incorporates Saxton's reminiscences from the Boston Evening Transcript, adding a letter of 3 April 1845 from his father about sending him to Brook Farm.

A 132 Saxton, S. Willard. "Last Remaining Brook Farmer (But One) Recalls Its Beauty," Boston Evening Transcript, 29 July 1916, Part 2, p. 4.

Saxton went to Brook Farm in 1844 at age fifteen and helped as a printer. His account contains valuable information on the Harbinger, on daily life at the community, on the burning of the Phalanstery, and on Charles A. Dana.

JOHN VAN DER ZEE SEARS

A 133 Sears, John Van Der Zee. My Friends at Brook Farm. New York: Desmond FitzGerald, 1912.

Sears was sent to Brook Farm when he was twelve and stayed until after the fire in 1846. His account is more anecdotal than factual. Coming from an upperclass

Dutch family in New York, Sears had a certain insularity
that originally set him apart from the other children,
but he soon settled in, though most of the book shows
its author to be rather superior and priggish towards
the proceedings at Brook Farm. One chapter deals with
Horace Greeley, a family friend. Illustrated.

Reviews:

"A Boy at Brook Farm," Independent, 74 (16 January 1913):
151-152. Sears has presented a "very pleasant picture"
of Brook Farm.
ALA Booklist, 9 (February 1913): 251. This book has "no
special literary merit but is interesting."
[Johnson, Rossiter.] Literary Digest, 46 (15 February
1913): 352. This is an "interesting sketch" written
in an "easy and entertaining" style.
Nation, 96 (20 February 1913): 184. This is an
"interesting" book, but lacks clarity because it gives
no dates, and has very one-sided character sketches.

ORA GANNETT SEDGWICK

A 134 Sedgwick, Ora Gannett. "A Girl of Sixteen at Brook Farm,"
Atlantic Monthly, 85 (March 1900): 394-404.

Sedgwick arrived at Brook Farm in June 1841 and stayed
for eighteen months. Her account contains information
on the school, Charles A. Dana, George William Curtis,
Isaac Hecker, and especially Hawthorne.

A 135 "'A Girl of Sixteen at Brook Farm,'" New York Times, 17
March 1900, p. 169.

Summarizes Sedgwick's article in the Atlantic Monthly.

ARTHUR SUMNER

A 136 Sumner, Arthur. "A Boy's Recollections of Brook Farm," New
England Magazine, 10 (May 1894): 309-313.

Sumner was sixteen when he arrived at Brook Farm during
its early days, and his recollections are vague and
general, with sketches of Ripley, Dwight, Charles A.
Dana, and George William Curtis. Sumner also describes
a picnic he believes Hawthorne used in The Blithedale
Romance.

SECTION B: VISITORS

VISITORS

ANONYMOUS

B 1   "The Community at West Roxbury, Mass.," Monthly Miscellany of Religion and Letters, 5 (August 1841): 113–118.

Prints a letter from an unidentified visitor to Brook Farm to a lady in England describing the founding and goals of the community.

ABIGAIL ALCOTT

B 2   The Journals of Bronson Alcott, ed. Odell Shepard. Boston: Little, Brown, 1938.

Mrs. Abigail Alcott's journal entry of 3 February 1844 describes a visit to Brook Farm, where she was impressed by its "neatness, order, beauty, and life," but she sees "but little gained in the association in labour" (p. 157).

AMOS BRONSON ALCOTT

B 3   The Letters of A. Bronson Alcott, ed. Richard L. Herrnstadt. Ames: Iowa State University Press, 1969.

Prints Alcott's letters of 24 February 1874 and 29 December 1875 in answer to people asking him for information about Brook Farm (pp. 626–627, 663).

ALBERT BRISBANE

B 4   Brisbane, Redelia. Albert Brisbane. A Mental Biography. Boston: Arena, 1893.

Brook Farm applied Fourier's ideas with "breadth and elevation" in an atmosphere of high "social and intellectual character." It failed because "it had been established without science, and without the means of applying principles concretely," and as a result, "the legitimate aspirations and ambitions of the individual found there no satisfying field of action (pp. 214–218).

B 5   Carlson, Oliver. Brisbane: A Candid Biography. New York: Stackpole Sons, 1937.

Brief account of Brook Farm and Albert Brisbane's connection with it (pp. 55-58).

ORESTES A. BROWNSON

B 6   Brownson, O.A. "Brook Farm," <u>United States Magazine and Democratic Review</u>, 11 (November 1842): 481-496.

Brownson prints a letter addressed to him by a "highly esteemed friend and distinguished literary lady" giving her favorable account of the community's goals, especially the educational methods, seen during her visit to Brook Farm that August, and prefaces it with his own positive comments on the community and its aims. The letter is reprinted as "The West-Roxbury Community," <u>New-York Daily Tribune</u>, 20 January 1843, p. 4.

B 7   [Brownson, Orestes A.] "Transcendentalism, or the latest Form of Infidelity," <u>Brownson's Quarterly Review</u>, 7 (July 1845): 273-323.

"A sweet young lady gave us one day as her reason for joining what is now a Fourier community, that she was disgusted with conventionalism, and wished to be free from its galling restraints, and to live in the simplicity of nature. Poor girl!"

B 8   Brownson, Henry F. <u>Orestes A. Brownson's Early Life: From 1803 to 1844</u>. Detroit: H.F. Brownson, 1898.

Describes Brownson's relations with Ripley and Brook Farm, printing letters of 28 November 1842 from Hugh A. Garland to Brownson prompted by the latter's article on Brook Farm in that month's <u>Democratic Review</u>, asking if Brownson would recommend sending his children to the Brook Farm school; of 18 December 1842 from Ripley to Brownson about the principles behind Brook Farm, and of 22 July 1843 about the progress of Brownson's eldest son in the Brook Farm school (pp. 306-316); and prints a letter of 7 January 1843 from John Hecker to Brownson about Isaac Hecker and his stay at Brook Farm (pp. 501-503). See also G 226-G 229.

B 9   McAvoy, Thomas T., and Lawrence J. Bradley. <u>Guide to the Microfilm Edition of the Orestes Augustus Brownson Papers</u>. Notre Dame: University of Notre Dame Archives, 1966.

Roll Two ("Correspondence, 1843-1849") contains "a number of letters bearing upon such matters as Albert Brisbane's Brook Farm experiment," including the originals of those letters published in Henry F. Brownson's life of his father (p. 17). See also G 226-G 231.

B 10   Maynard, Theodore. <u>Orestes Brownson: Yankee, Radical, Catholic</u>. New York: Macmillan, 1943.

> Brownson never completely identified with Brook Farm because he was too individualistic, even if he had not been put off by the Brook Farmers' ignorance of "the patent fact of original sin" (pp. 108-115).

B 11   Schlesinger, Arthur M., Jr. <u>Orestes A. Brownson: A Pilgrim's Progress</u>. Boston: Little, Brown, 1939.

> Brownson's relationship with Brook Farm became strained because he was "too religious for them." By 1842 Brownson had "too intense and concrete a belief to fraternize with people who ignored evil, [and] sputtered about the infinite and generalized their vagueness into the universe" (pp. 150-155).

B 12   Sveino, Per. <u>Orestes A. Brownson's Road to Catholicism</u>. New York: Humanities Press, 1970.

> Discusses the "positive response to his Catholizing tendencies" which Brownson found at Brook Farm (pp. 279-281).

B 13   Whalen, Doran. "Brook Farm," in his <u>Granite for God's House: The Life of Orestes Augustus Brownson</u>, pp. 143-157. New York: Sheed & Ward, 1941.

> General account of the community, over-emphasizing Brownson's loose connection with it.

JOHN A. COLLINS

B 14   C. "Brook Farm," <u>Communitist</u>, 1 (21 August 1844): 26.

> When the writer visited the community six weeks earlier, he found it had 115 persons and was in "a flourishing condition." "C." is probably John A. Collins, leader of the Skaneateles community in New York, which published the <u>Communitist</u>.

B 15   C. "Fourierism," <u>Communitist</u>, 1 (23 April 1845): 91.

> Favorable description of the Brook Farm Phalanx.

ROBERT CARTER

B 16   Carter, Robert. "The 'Newness,'" <u>Century Magazine</u>, n.s. 39 (November 1889): 124-131.

> Brief, uninformative comments on Brook Farm, partially based on Carter's one-day visit there.

WILLIAM HENRY CHANNING

B 17 [Channing, William Henry.] "The Fountain in the Palace," Harbinger, 1 (21 June 1845): 24-25.

"A Story told to the Brook Farm Children at the Crowning of their Summer Queen, June 2."

B 18 [Channing, William Henry.] "Signs of the Times. Brook Farm Association," Present, 1 (1 March 1844): 350-353.

The introduction to the Brook Farm Constitution is reprinted, with the Present calling the occasion "cause for rejoicing."

B 19 Frothingham, Octavius Brooks. Memoir of William Henry Channing. Boston: Houghton, Mifflin, 1886.

Prints Channing's letters of 13 January 1870 to J.H. Noyes correcting some of the latter's errors about Brook Farm in his History of American Socialisms (D 66); of 25 December 1845 to Marcus Spring, of 8 November 1846 to Dwight, and of 10-11 March 1846 to an unnamed friend, all giving his positive feelings about the community and its goals (pp. 209-219).

CHRISTOPHER PEARSE CRANCH

B 20 [Curtis, George William.] "Editor's Easy Chair," Harper's New Monthly Magazine, 84 (April 1892): 800-801.

Brief description of Cranch at Brook Farm.

B 21 Scott, Leonora Cranch. The Life and Letters of Christopher Pearse Cranch. Boston: Houghton Mifflin, 1917.

Prints Cranch's letters of 30 May 1843 to his brother about the possibility of his going to Brook Farm to live after his marriage, and of 8 April 1844 to Dwight about the latter's devotion to reform (pp. 81, 88-89).

RALPH WALDO EMERSON

B 22 The Correspondence of Emerson and Carlyle, ed. Joseph Slater. New York: Columbia University Press, 1964.

Prints Emerson's letter of 30 October 1840 stating: "George Ripley is taking up a colony of agriculturalists & scholars with whom he threatens to take the field & the book" (p. 284).

B 23 Emerson, Ralph Waldo. "Historic Notes of Life and Letters in Massachusetts," Atlantic Monthly, 52 (October 1883): 529-543.

One reason for Brook Farm's failure was its lack of any central authority. Reprinted as "Historic Notes of Life and Letters in New England," in <u>Lectures and Biographical Sketches</u> in <u>The Complete Works of Ralph Waldo Emerson</u>, 12 vols. (Boston: Houghton, Mifflin, 1903-1904), 10:323-370.

B 24 <u>The Journals and Miscellaneous Notebooks of Ralph Waldo Emerson</u>, ed. William H. Gilman et al. 14 vols. to date. Cambridge: Harvard University Press, 1960- .

Prints Emerson's important comments on Brook Farm, especially throughout volumes 8 and 9. This edition supersedes the 1909-1914 edition of Emerson's <u>Journals</u> published by Houghton Mifflin.

B 25 <u>The Letters of Ralph Waldo Emerson</u>, ed. Ralph L. Rusk. 6 vols. New York: Columbia University Press, 1939.

Valuable references to Brook Farm throughout.

B 26 "Mr. Emerson's Third Lecture," <u>National Anti-Slavery Standard</u>, 31 October 1868, p. 2.

Brief, uninformative account of Emerson's lecture on Brook Farm. Reprinted in Kenneth Walter Cameron, <u>Transcendental Log</u> (Hartford: Transcendental Books, 1973), p. 199.

B 27 Boynton, Percy H. "Emerson's Feelings Toward Reform," <u>New Republic</u>, 1 (30 January 1915): 16-18.

Emerson's self-reliance made him announce that sympathy with a good cause did not "invoke partnership in it." This is especially true of his relations with Brook Farm.

B 28 Cabot, James Elliot. <u>A Memoir of Ralph Waldo Emerson</u>. 2 vols. Boston: Houghton, Mifflin, 1887.

Briefly summarizes Emerson's thoughts on Brook Farm, as seen in his manuscript letters and journals (2:434-442). Superseded by new editions of Emerson's writings, especially the <u>Letters</u> (B 25) and <u>Journals and Miscellaneous Notebooks</u> (B 24).

B 29 Cameron, Kenneth Walter. "A Bundle of Emerson Letters," <u>Emerson Society Quarterly</u>, No. 22 (I Quarter 1961): 95-97.

In a letter of 20 April 1845 to Dwight, first published with inaccuracies in G.W. Cooke's biography of Dwight (A 44), Emerson answers a request to contribute to the <u>Harbinger</u>: "As far as your journal is sectarian, I shall respect it at a distance; if it should become catholic, I shall be found suing for a place in it" (95-96).

B 30   Conway, Moncure Daniel. "A Six Years' Day-Dream," in his
        Emerson at Home and Abroad, pp. 194-208. Boston: James
        R. Osgood, 1882.

        General account of the community, drawn mainly from
        Hawthorne's writings.

B 31   Firkins, O.W. Ralph Waldo Emerson. Boston: Houghton
        Mifflin, 1915.

        Brief summary of Emerson's reasons for not joining
        Brook Farm (pp. 101-105).

B 32   Flanagan, John T. "Emerson and Communism," New England
        Quarterly, 10 (June 1937): 243-261.

        Emerson's "doctrine of individualism," his belief in the
        necessity for inner reform before social reform, and his
        unwillingness to disturb the status quo form the basis
        of his refusal to join Brook Farm.

B 33   Garnett, Richard. Life of Ralph Waldo Emerson. London:
        Walter Scott, 1888.

        Defends Emerson's decision not to join Brook Farm, which
        Garnett calls "little more than an intellectual picnic"
        (pp. 104-106).

B 34   Matle, John H. "Emerson and Brook Farm," Emerson Society
        Quarterly, No. 58 (I Quarter 1970): 84-88.

        Emerson's individualism kept him from joining Brook Farm.

B 35   Snider, Denton J. A Biography of Ralph Waldo Emerson. St.
        Louis: William Harvey Miner, 1921.

        Examines Emerson's reasons--"a very real and serious
        conflict"--for not joining Brook Farm (pp. 265-270).

JOHN FINCH

B 36   Finch, John. "Correspondence," New Moral World [England],
        12 (13 January 1844): 232.

        Finch states in his letter of 23 December 1843 that he
        has visited Brook Farm, which he discovered to be "a
        superior educational establishment, where farming,
        gardening, and some useful trades are taught."

B 37   Finch, John. "Notes of Travel in the United States," New
        Moral World [England], 12 (13 April 1844): 329.

        In his letter of 10 April 1844, Finch describes his
        visit to Brook Farm the previous May, concluding that

"from the knowledge, zeal, diligence, good feeling, cleanliness, and order everywhere seen, there is not the least reason to doubt of its complete success."

MARGARET FULLER

B 38   Brown, Arthur W. <u>Margaret Fuller</u>. New York: Twayne, 1964.

   Good description of Fuller's visits to Brook Farm (pp. 62–67).

B 39   [Curtis, George William.] "Editor's Easy Chair," <u>Harper's New Monthly Magazine</u>, 64 (March 1882): 627–628.

   Recollections of Fuller and her visits to Brook Farm.

B 40   [Emerson, Ralph Waldo, William Henry Channing, and James Freeman Clarke.] <u>Memoirs of Margaret Fuller Ossoli</u>. 2 vols. Boston: Phillips, Sampson, 1852.

   Prints comments on Brook Farm from Fuller's journals and letters showing "While at heart sympathizing with the heroism that prompted it, in judgment she considered it premature" (2:72–79).

B 41   Higginson, Thomas Wentworth. "Brook Farm," in his <u>Margaret Fuller Ossoli</u>, pp. 173–186. Boston: Houghton, Mifflin, 1884.

   Important description of the community, drawing upon manuscript letters, primarily aimed at refuting the charge that Hawthorne portrayed Fuller as Zenobia in <u>The Blithedale Romance</u>.

B 42   Hudspeth, Robert N. "A Calendar of the Letters of Margaret Fuller," <u>Studies in the American Renaissance 1977</u>, ed. Joel Myerson, pp. 48–143. Boston: Twayne, 1978.

   This chronological list of Fuller's letters, including those written from Brook Farm, gives the present location of manuscript letters and the printing history for all letters. Especially valuable for using the Brook Farm letters printed in the <u>Memoirs</u>.

B 43   Knortz, Karl. <u>Brook Farm und Margaret Fuller</u>. New York: Druck von Hermann Bartsch, 1886. [German]

   General account of the community and Fuller's involvement in it.

B 44   Stern, Madeleine B. <u>The Life of Margaret Fuller</u>. New York: Dutton, 1942.

Reconstruction of Fuller's visits to Brook Farm (pp. 237-265).

RICHARD FULLER

B 45   Recollections of Richard F. Fuller. Boston: Privately printed, 1936.

   A major fault of Brook Farm, as Fuller remembers from his visits there, was that "they did not sufficiently regard the family circle" (p. 80).

HORACE GREELEY

B 46   Michael, Cecelia Koretsky. "Horace Greeley and Fourierism in the United States." M.A. thesis, University of Rochester, 1949. 156 pp.

   Excellent discussion of Greeley's support of Fourierism, especially as seen in the pages of the New-York Tribune.

B 47   Southeran, Charles. Horace Greeley and Other Pioneers of American Socialism. New York: Humboldt, 1892.

   General account of Brook Farm and its members, especially their relations with Greeley and the New-York Tribune (pp. 282-295).

B 48   Stoddard, Henry Luther. "The Brook Farmers: Dana and Margaret Fuller," in his Horace Greeley, pp. 95-104. New York: Putnams, 1946.

   Discusses Greeley's relations with Charles A. Dana, Fuller, and Brook Farm.

B 49   "A Guest." "Celebration of Fourier's Birth Day at Brook Farm," Phalanx, 1 (3 May 1845): 336-337.

   Description of the festivities.

A. BLOOMER HART

B 50   H[art]., A. B[loomer]. "Brook Farm," Phalanx, 1 (27 July 1844): 220-221.

   Favorable description of the "moral triumph" of the community as seen by Hart during his recent visit there.

THOMAS WENTWORTH HIGGINSON

B 51 Higginson, Tho[ma]s. Wentworth. "The Brook Farm Period in New England," <u>Demorest's Monthly Magazine</u>, 18 (July 1882): 534-535.

    A description of the air of intellectual excitement in the 1840s, and of Higginson's visits to the community.

B 52 Higginson, Thomas Wentworth. <u>Cheerful Yesterdays</u>. Boston: Houghton, Mifflin, 1898.

    General reminiscences of the Brook Farmers' visits to Boston, and of Higginson's own two visits to the community (pp. 83-86).

B 53 <u>Letters and Journals of Thomas Wentworth Higginson 1846-1906</u>, ed. Mary Thacher Higginson. Boston: Houghton Mifflin, 1921.

    Prints Higginson's letter of May 1854 [sic] discussing Charles A. Dana's decision to leave Brook Farm (pp. 13-14).

B 54 Higginson, Mary Thacher. <u>Thomas Wentworth Higginson</u>. Boston: Houghton Mifflin, 1914.

    Prints Higginson's journal entry describing a visit to Brook Farm (pp. 48-49).

JAMES HOSMER

B 55 Hosmer, James Kendall. <u>The Last Leaf</u>. New York: Putnams, 1912.

    As a child, Hosmer visited Brook Farm with his father. He recalls that at dinner Ripley placed his father next to Hawthorne with this comment: "I shall not introduce you, Mr. Hawthorne prefers not to be introduced to people" (p. 240).

FREDERIC DAN HUNTINGTON

B 56 Huntington, Arria S. <u>Memoir and Letters of Frederic Dan Huntington</u>. Boston: Houghton, Mifflin, 1906.

    Prints Huntington's letter of 19 July 1842 to his brother describing briefly his visit to Brook Farm, which he came away from with a feeling of "sadness and commiseration," and gives his comments on the community made forty years later (pp. 68-70).

JAMES KAY

B 57 Gohdes, Clarence. "Three Letters by James Kay Dealing With Brook Farm," Philological Quarterly, 17 (October 1938): 377-388.

Kay was a frequent visitor to Brook Farm and his son was enrolled in the school. Printed here are letters to Dwight of 14 March 1845 discussing the planned reorganization of Brook Farm along Fourierist principles, and of 10 May 1846 offering general advice; and of 27 September 1846 to Marianne Dwight suggesting ways to save the community from disintegration in the face of its diminishing funds.

CHARLES LANE

B 58 Lane, Charles. "American Correspondence," New Age, Concordium Gazette, and Temperance Advocate [England], 1 (1 September 1843): 90.

Prints Lane's letter of 30 July 1843 to the editor describing his and Bronson Alcott's visits to Brook Farm, a community where people are "playing away their youth and day-time in a miserably joyous frivolous manner." Lane had founded the Fruitlands community with Alcott, and his own ascetic tastes influenced his comments on Brook Farm.

B 59 L[ane]., C[harles]. "Brook Farm," Dial, 4 (January 1844): 351-357.

Brook Farm, "though sufficiently extensive in respect to number of persons, is not to be considered an experiment of large intent" because it is "merely an aggregation of persons, and lacks that oneness of spirit, which is probably needful to make it of deep and lasting value to mankind." Lane sees three types of people at Brook Farm: those who believe "an improved state of existence would be developed in association," those who "join with the view of bettering their condition, by being exempted from some portion of worldly strife," and those who "have their own development or education, for their principal object." Yet, though Brook Farm's "aims are moderate," it may succeed because it does not attempt too much.

ELIZABETH PALMER PEABODY

B 60 P[eabody]., E[lizabeth]. P[almer].. "Fourierism," Dial, 4 (April 1844): 473-483.

Peabody favorably describes Fourierism and announces that Brook Farm has become a Fourierist establishment, which gives her cause to "rejoice." Reprinted in her <u>Last Evening with Allston, and Other Papers</u> (Boston: D. Lothrop, 1886), pp. 202-216.

B 61 [Peabody, Elizabeth Palmer.] "A Glimpse of Christ's Idea of Society," <u>Dial</u>, 2 (October 1841): 214-228.

This article, relating Christ's teachings to social organizations, is introductory to Peabody's account of Brook Farm in the January 1842 <u>Dial</u>. Reprinted as "Brook Farm Interpretation of Christ's Idea of Society," in her <u>Last Evening with Allston, and Other Papers</u> (Boston: D. Lothrop, 1886), pp. 181-201.

B 62 P[eabody]., E[lizabeth]. P[almer]. "Plan of the West Roxbury Community," <u>Dial</u>, 2 (January 1842): 361-372.

Favorable and important attempt at describing the methods of the Brook Farmers. Peabody sees two possible problems arising from the experiment, "antagonism" and "the spirit of coterie," but sees them overcome by "Love" and "transcendentalism" or "the common ground to which all sects may rise, and be purified of their narrowness." Reprinted as "The West-Roxbury Community. (Near Boston.)," <u>New-York Weekly Tribune</u>, 22 January 1842, p. 1, and <u>New-York Daily Tribune</u>, 28 January 1842, p. 4.

M. E. W. SHERWOOD

B 63 Sherwood, M.E.W. <u>An Epistle to Posterity Being Rambling Recollections of Many Years of My Life</u>. New York: Harpers, 1897.

General recollections of Sherwood's brief visit to Brook Farm in its later years (pp. 36-37).

ELIZABETH CADY STANTON

B 64 Stanton, Elizabeth Cady. <u>Eighty Years and More (1815-1897)</u>. London: T. Fisher Unwin, 1898.

Brief account of a visit to Brook Farm, where Stanton felt the "charming family of intelligent men and women" had realized "Edward Bellamy's beautiful vision of the equal conditions of the human family in the year 2000" (pp. 134-135).

GEORGE LUTHER STEARNS

B 65 Stearns, Frank Preston. <u>The Life and Public Services of George Luther Stearns</u>. Philadelphia: Lippincott, 1907.

Stearns' account of Convers Francis' visit to Brook Farm in November 1842, from which he concluded that Ripley had "undertaken a madcap enterprise" (pp. 45-46).

GILES B. STEBBINS

B 66 Stebbins, Giles B. Upward Steps of Seventy Years. New York: United States Book Company, 1890.

Brief description of a visit to Brook Farm when the author was in his teens, when he was impressed by "the incongruity" of "the ploughman and the scholar oddly put together" there (pp. 53-54).

SECTION C: CONTEMPORARIES

CONTEMPORARIES

ANONYMOUS

C 1   "Agricultural School," New England Farmer and Horticultural Register, 19 (27 January 1841): 238-239.

Favorable account of the proposed community, here called the "Practical Institute of Agriculture and Education."

C 2   "Brook Farm," New-York Weekly Tribune, 2 May 1846, p. 1.

Friendly mention of the Brook Farm school and the Harbinger, designed to gain students for the school after the fire which destroyed the Phalanstery.

C 3   "Brook Farm," Phalanx, 1 (7 October 1844): 281.

Brief summary of the second edition of the Brook Farm Constitution.

C 4   "Brook Farm," Phalanx, 1 (9 December 1844): 304-306.

Partially reprints the second edition of the Brook Farm Constitution.

C 5   "The Brook Farm Association," Phalanx, 1 (5 February 1844): 68.

Notes with favor the reorganization of the community from "an educational establishment mainly, to a regularly organized Association."

C 6   "Brook Farm Phalanx," Phalanx, 1 (28 May 1845): 343-348.

Reprints the Constitution of the Brook Farm Phalanx.

C 7   "Constitution of the Brook Farm Association," Phalanx, 1 (1 March 1844): 80-82.

Reprints the first edition of the Brook Farm Constitution.

C 8   "Mistakes Corrected," New-York Daily Tribune, 24 August 1847, p. 2.

Despite a statement in the New-York Observer that Brook Farm has been disbanded, it is still functioning. However,

the community, "having been started without capital,
experience or industrial capacity, without reference to
or knowledge of Fourier's or any other systematic plan
of Association, on a most unfavorable locality, bought
at a high price, and constantly under mortgage . . . is
about to dissolve."

C 9   "Notes," Boston Evening Transcript, 3 November 1894, p. 12.

Prints a letter from C. Braxton about his unsuccessful
attempt, encouraged by the Brook Farmers, to put the
"general idea" of Brook Farm to work in a Boston
boardinghouse.

C 10 "The Roxbury Community," Phalanx, 1 (5 October 1843): 15-16.

Brief description of the "Educational establishment"
which has the best school in the country.

C 11 "The West Roxbury Community," New-York Weekly Tribune,
25 February 1843, p. 2.

Positive description of the "peculiarities of Education"
at Brook Farm.

C 12 Carlyle, Thomas. Past and Present. Boston: Charles C.
Little and James Brown, 1843.

"A strange, chill, almost ghastly dayspring strikes
up in Yankeeland itself: my Transcendental friends
announce there, in a distinct though somewhat lankhaired
ungainly manner, that the Demiurgus Dollar is dethroned
. . . Socinian preachers quit their pulpits in
Yankeeland . . . and retire into the fields to cultivate
onion-beds, and live frugally on vegetables" (p. 294).
This is undoubtedly a reference to Ripley's leaving the
ministry for Brook Farm.

C 13 Dall, Caroline. Transcendentalism in New England: A Lecture.
Boston: Roberts, 1897.

Brief comments on Brook Farm by one who was "offered the
position of dairy maid" by Ripley but refused, believing
the project "a chimera" (pp. 26-29).

C 14 Caleb and Mary Wilder Foote: Reminiscences and Letters, ed.
Mary Wilder Tileston. Boston: Houghton Mifflin, 1918.

Prints Mrs. Foote's letters of 2 March 1845 expressing
her belief that the Brook Farmers could do more good
by working their "elevating influence" in Boston (pp.
121-122), and of 2 November 1845, recalling Mrs. David

Mack's "quite entertaining" sketch of Brook Farm in a recent letter, which nevertheless reinforces the reasons for Mrs. Foote's "little faith" in the community (pp. 124-125).

FOURIERISM

C 15 Charles Fourier's ideas were made known to the American public mainly through the writings of Albert Brisbane, whose major works were: Social Destiny of Man: or Association and Reorganization of Industry (Philadelphia: C.F. Stollmeyer, 1840); "On Association and Attractive Industry," United States Magazine and Democratic Review, n.s. 10 (January, February, April, June 1842): 30-44, 167-182, 321-336, 560-580; and Association; or, A Concise Exposition of the Practical Part of Fourier's Social Science (New York: Greeley & McElrath, 1843), also published as A Concise Exposition of the Doctrine of Association (New York: J.S. Redfield, 1843). Also of use is Parke Godwin, A Popular View of the Doctrines of Charles Fourier (New York: J.S. Redfield, 1844). A good modern study of Fourier is Nicholas V. Riasanovsky, The Teaching of Charles Fourier (Berkeley: University of California Press, 1969).

C 16 Jordan, John W. "Two Interesting Emerson Letters," Book-Lover, No. 18 (May-June 1903): 118.

Prints a letter of 27 October 1842 by Thomas Carlyle expressing his "total, deep, irreclaimable dissent" from "a certain set of persons" in New England "grounding themselves on these ideas of Emerson's," who "are already about renouncing this miserable humbug of a world altogether, and retiring into the rural wilderness, to live there exclusively upon vegetables raised by their own digging."

C 17 The Letters of Henry Wadsworth Longfellow, ed. Andrew Hilen. 4 vols. to date. Cambridge: Harvard University Press, 1966- .

Prints Longfellow's letter of 18 October 1840 announcing what he has heard about Ripley's plans for going to Brook Farm (2:257).

C 18 Coleridge's American Disciples: The Selected Correspondence of James Marsh, ed. John J. Duffy. Amherst: University of Massachusetts Press, 1973.

Prints Ripley's letter of 17 October 1840 about his plans for Brook Farm (p. 240), and reprints Marsh's letter of

1 March 1841 expressing his skepticism about the community from Wells, Three Christian Transcendentalists (C 26) (pp. 254-255).

C 19 Moss, Sidney P. Poe's Literary Battles. Durham: Duke University Press, 1963.

Good summary of Poe's brief feud with the Harbinger (pp. 204-206).

C 20 Myerson, Joel. "'A True & High Minded Person': Transcendentalist Sarah Clarke," Southwest Review, 59 (Spring 1974): 163-172.

Prints Clarke's letter of 6 December 1840 describing Ripley's preliminary plans for establishing his community (169-170).

C 21 Peabody, Elizabeth Palmer. Reminiscences of Rev. Wm. Ellery Channing, D.D. Boston: Roberts, 1880.

Channing looked on Ripley's community with "interest and favor, although he had a thousand doubts about its immediate success" (pp. 405-407, 418-419).

THE PHALANX

C 22 The Phalanx, subtitled "Journal of Social Science, Devoted to the Cause of Association or a Social Reform and the Elevation of the Human Race," published twenty-three numbers in one volume between 5 October 1843 and 28 May 1845, when it was replaced by the Harbinger. Besides articles dealing directly with Brook Farm, listed elsewhere, the following articles provide useful background information: "What is Association?" 1 (5 January, 4 May 1844): 56-58, 131-132, printed as "an excellent thing for country papers to copy to give their readers a familiar view of the subject"; and "Address," 1 (20 April 1844): 107-113, which prints the address to the public of the "General Convention of the Friends of Association in the United States," pointing out what the associationists felt was wrong with society and how they proposed to correct these ills.

C 23 Pierce, Edward L. Memoir and Letters of Charles Sumner. 2 vols. Boston: Roberts, 1877.

Prints Sumner's letters of 16 September 1842 and 15 May 1844 about the positive results of his brother Horace's move to Brook Farm (2:224, 306), and describes a discussion in which Sumner disagrees with the goals of the community (2:294-295).

C 24 [Poe, Edgar Allan.] "Editorial Miscellany," Broadway Journal, 2 (13 December 1845): 357–358.

The Harbinger is "the most reputable organ of the Crazyites." This is seen especially in its negative review of Poe's The Raven and Other Poems.

C 25 Tiffany, Nina Moore and Francis. Harm Jan Huidekoper. Cambridge: Riverside Press, 1904.

Prints Huidekoper's letters to his daughter (Mrs. James Freeman Clarke) of 18 August and 16 September 1841, remarking with gentle irony on Brook Farm (pp. 288–289).

C 26 Wells, Roland Vale. Three Christian Transcendentalists: James Marsh, Caleb Sprague Henry, Frederic Henry Hedge. New York: Columbia University Press, 1943.

Prints Marsh's letter of 1 March 1841 expressing his skepticism about Brook Farm (pp. 166–167). Reprinted in Marsh's Correspondence (C 18).

C 27 The Letters of John Greenleaf Whittier, ed. John B. Pickard. 3 vols. Cambridge: Harvard University Press, 1975.

Whittier's letter of 1 March 1847 to the National Era complains that the Harbinger has taken exception to his comments on associationism as printed in the 11 February issue (2:80–81).

SECTION D: HISTORIES

HISTORIES

D 1   "Brook Farm," <u>Bulletin of the Salem Public Library</u>, 6 (February 1903): 143.

    Uninformative list of books and articles on Brook Farm at the Salem Public Library.

D 2   "Brook Farm. A Social Enterprise," unidentified newspaper, 25 April 1874.

    Uninformative, general comments on the community. Reprinted in Kenneth Walter Cameron, <u>Transcendental Log</u> (Hartford: Transcendental Books, 1973), pp. 273-274.

D 3   "'Brook Farm' in 1896," <u>Boston Evening Transcript</u>, 10 March 1896, p. 6.

    Description of the current state of the buildings and grounds.

D 4   [Adams, Raymond.] <u>Brook Farm 1841-1941. Books from the Shelves of Raymond Adams. An Exhibit at the University of North Carolina Library, November, 1941</u>. Mimeographed. [Chapel Hill: n.p., 1941].

    Exhibition catalogue of books and articles dealing with Brook Farm and communitarianism.

D 5   Alberti, Charles Edward. "Brook Farm's Educational Philosophy (1841-1846): A Study into its Methods, Axiology and Epistemology." Ph.D. dissertation, Loyola University of Chicago, 1975. 210 pp.

    General survey of the community's educational ideas.

D 6   [Arnold, William Harris.] "The Unitarian Spring at Brook Farm," <u>Proceedings of the Unitarian Historical Society</u>, 7 (1942): 1-10.

    Uninformative account of the community.

D 7   Bates, Ernest Sutherland. <u>American Faith</u>. New York: Norton, 1940.

    Brook Farm was "unique among the co-operative movements" in its "preservation of individual cultural values in the midst of its socializing aims." The introduction of Fourierism was "wholly disastrous," and the "happy spontaneity, the atmosphere of free discussion and inquiry disappeared" (pp. 378-381, 387-388).

D 8   Bestor, Arthur E., Jr. Brook Farm 1841-1847. An Exhibition to Commemorate the Centenary of Its Founding. Mimeographed. [New York]: Columbia University Libraries, 1941.

Brief history of the community and checklist of books, periodicals, manuscripts, and illustrated material on display.

D 9   Bestor, Arthur E., Jr. "Fourierism in Northampton: A Critical Note," New England Quarterly, 13 (March 1940): 110-122.

Relations between the non-Fourierist Northampton Association and Brook Farm, friendly at first, gradually cooled as the West Roxbury community modelled itself more and more on Fourier's doctrines.

D 10 Bonham, Martha E. "The 'Brave New World' of Brook Farm," Scholastic, 39 (29 September 1941): 18-19.

Uninformative account of the community; illustrated.

D 11 Boughton, Willis. Syllabus of a Course of Six Lectures on the Brook Farm Community. University Extension Lectures under the Auspices of the American Society for the Extension of University Teaching. Series A. No. 22. [Philadelphia: American Society for the Extension of University Teaching, 1892].

Lecture outlines, readings, references, and exercises on the community, its visitors, and its members.

D 12 Brook Farm Centennial Committee. Brook Farm: The Story of the Historic Social Experiment 1841-1847. West Roxbury: Brook Farm Centennial Committee, 1941.

Brief, uninformative account of the community; illustrated.

D 13 Brooks, Van Wyck. The Flowering of New England 1815-1865. New York: Dutton, 1936.

General, impressionistic account of Brook Farm (pp. 242-251).

D 14 Brooks, Van Wyck. "Retreat from Utopia," Saturday Review of Literature, 13 (22 February 1936): 3-4, 14, 16, 18.

Prints a chapter later included in Brooks' The Flowering of New England.

D 15 Burton, Katherine. Paradise Planters: The Story of Brook Farm. London: Longmans, Green, 1939.

Despite her disclaimer that "I have tried to keep this book fact and not fiction," Burton's work must be classified as a novel and not as a scholarly study. It is replete with factual errors, overbearing with a cloying sentimentalism, and marred by a disregard for accuracy. Her conversational technique involves placing words from their writings, letters, and journals into the mouths of real people and the result is disastrous, since she usually uses these writings out of context. This book is more dangerous, because of its errors and unsupported assumptions, than it is helpful. If used at all, it should be used with extreme caution, and not without a careful crosschecking of Burton's facts.

Reviews:

R., W.K. "Brook Farm," Christian Science Monitor, 1 March 1939, p. 16. This account contains "warmth and vitality," chiefly through its use of reconstructed conversations.

Shepard, Odell. "Interpreting Brook Farm," Saturday Review of Literature, 19 (11 March 1939): 7. "With little concern for chronology and with scant attention to continuity of thought or of topic," Burton has manipulated her materials into "a pattern of events which has slight discernible resemblance to what actually went on at Brook Farm." Burton's reply to this review is "'Paradise Planters,'" Saturday Review of Literature, 19 (15 April 1939): 9.

D., R.T. "Out in West Roxbury," Boston Evening Transcript, 18 March 1939, Section 4, p. 1. Despite occasional factual errors and "wooden" characters, Burton's "deep sympathy and admiration" for the Brook Farmers make her book interesting.

Marsh, Fred T. "'Earthly Paradise on a Rough New England Pasture,'" New York Times Book Review, 19 March 1939, p. 3. This is "a wholly delightful and utterly honest book."

Wisconsin Library Bulletin, 35 (April 1939): 60. The conversational form of presentation gives the book "the appearance of fiction."

McS[orley]., J[oseph]. Catholic World, 149 (April 1939): 120-121. This book makes an "acceptable contribution" to the literature on its subject.

ALA Booklist, 35 (1 April 1939): 245. Burton's book is "sympathetically" written.

"Brook Farm Colony and its Transients," Springfield Republican, 2 April 1939, p. 7e. Burton's

fictionalized account of Brook Farm succeeds in
bringing characters to life.
New Republic, 98 (5 April 1939): 259. The recreated
conversations fail to produce "convincing characters."
Eaton, Walter Prichard. Commonweal, 30 (26 May 1939):
134. This book starts slowly but is highly animated
when it deals with the daily activities of the Brook
Farmers.
Stillman, Clara Gruening. "A Little Group of Serious
Doers," Books [New York Herald Tribune], 18 June 1939,
p. 2. Burton has presented, especially by her
conversational technique, a "most entertaining account"
of Brook Farm.
Times Literary Supplement, 22 July 1939, p. 443. This
history of the community is told with "understanding
and knowledge."
Geismar, Maxwell. "Fine Talk," Nation, 149 (12 August
1939): 177-178. Although Burton's conversational
method is suspect, she has created a lively picture
of Brook Farm.
Christian Century, 56 (16 August 1939): 998. This
"careful study" is "almost fictionalized," but
nevertheless gives a good balanced view of the
community.
Hislop, Codman. New England Quarterly, 13 (March 1940):
136-138. Burton's "picture-evoking pattern" is "keyed
to the popular mind she wants to reach."

D 16 Calverton, V.F. "Brook Farm," in his Where Angels Dared to
Tread, pp. 197-224. Indianapolis: Bobbs-Merrill, 1941.

General account of the community, noting the sharp
decline of enthusiasm by the original members when
Fourierism took over.

D 17 Carew, Harold D. "'Bolsheviks,' Old Style," Bookman, 68
(February 1929): 630-638.

Fictionalized reconstruction of Brook Farm and its period.

D 18 Clark, Jerome L. 1844. 3 vols. Nashville: Southern
Publishing Association, 1968.

Of all the "cooperative colonies," Brook Farm was "the
one most interested in cultural values for their own
sake." The "Fourierist fiasco" ruined this "intellectual
stimulation" (2:190-196).

D 19 Cooke, George Willis. "Brook Farm," New England Magazine,
n.s. 17 (December 1897): 391-407.

Good general account of the community; illustrated.

D 20   Crawford, Mary C. "The Brook Farmers," in her The Romance of Old New England Rooftrees, pp. 293–306. Boston: L.C. Page, 1902.

General account of the community; illustrated.

D 21   Crowe, Charles R. "Fourierism and the Founding of Brook Farm," Boston Public Library Quarterly, 12 (April 1960): 79–88.

An examination of Ripley's career shows that the basic principles of Fourierism were already in his mind when he started Brook Farm. The goals of the "associationist" Brook Farm differ little from the aims of the Fourierist Brook Farm.

D 22   Crowe, Charles R. "'This Unnatural Union of Phalansteries and Transcendentalists,'" Journal of the History of Ideas, 20 (October–December 1959): 495–502.

The Brook Farmers' attempt to reconcile Transcendental individualism and Fourierist socialism, while not totally successful, was an important effort to solve "some of the most pressing cultural problems" of the period: "how shall industrial labor be made 'attractive'; how shall the problem of personality alienation among those in routine industrial and clerical occupations be overcome; how can the social isolation of so many in an impersonal industrial society be alleviated; how shall men and women be given a sense of participation, ownership, and interest in their occupations, communities, and nations; how can a social climate be created which makes it possible for individualists to thrive in a mass society?"

D 23   Crowe, Charles R. "Transcendentalist Support of Brook Farm: A Paradox?" Historian, 21 (May 1959): 281–295.

The apparent paradox between Transcendental individualism and Brook Farm communitarianism can partially be resolved. The "emotional coldness and the sense of social isolation" which so often characterized the personal lives of the Transcendentalists found relief in the intimacy of Brook Farm. Also, by the early 1840s many Transcendentalists were beginning to feel that complete individual liberty would have to be trimmed back for the greater end of social and cultural equality.

D 24   Crowe, Charles R. "Utopian Socialism in Rhode Island 1845–1850," Rhode Island History, 18 (January 1959): 20–26.

Describes the favorable impact made by lecturers from Brook Farm during the period indicated.

D 25 Curtis, Edith Roelker. "A Season in Utopia," American Heritage, 10 (April 1959): 58–63, 98–100.

General account of the community; illustrated.

D 26 Curtis, Edith Roelker. A Season in Utopia: The Story of Brook Farm. New York: Thomas Nelson, 1961.

Curtis' book is a popularized history of Brook Farm casting Albert Brisbane and Horace Greeley as the villains because, in Curtis' view, they made Ripley falsely believe they were behind the community, only to desert Brook Farm for the North American Phalanx. To someone who has not read anything else on Brook Farm, this can be an interesting history if used with caution. The book is full of minor inaccuracies: Curtis gets names and dates wrong, and habitually mistitles contemporary books and articles. More dangerous, she often mistakes her own assumptions about events at Brook Farm for facts and reports them as such. To a scholar this book is of limited value since what Curtis has done, in essence, is to string together previously published accounts of the community into a disjointed and impressionistic narrative. She has exercised little selectivity, resulting in large portions of the book being taken directly from Hawthorne's notebooks and The Blithedale Romance and from Marianne Dwight's Letters from Brook Farm. Of value is her use of the previously unlocated correspondence of William Allen concerning Brook Farm, and of Isaac Hecker's unpublished correspondence with Brook Farmers.

Reviews:

Haverstick, Iola. "Plain Living, High Thinking," New York Times Book Review, 3 December 1961, p. 56. This book has too much detail, no new information, and lacks life.

Sharp, Nancy Weatherly. "An Experiment in Group Living," This World [San Francisco Chronicle], 24 December 1961, p. 17. The history of Brook Farm is "thoroughly discussed" by Curtis.

Foster, Charles H. "Hawthorne Soon Began to Crumble," Christian Science Monitor, 4 January 1962, p. 11. Curtis' book is "the best study of the subject anyone has yet furnished," and corrects some of Swift's "sentimentality and prudential regard for notable reputations" in his book.

Schlueter, Paul. "Nostalgic Approach," Christian Century, 79 (9 May 1962): 601. The value of this book is severely limited by its "lack of precision in documentation."

School and Society, 90 (6 October 1962): 316. This is a "conscientious, well-written account" of Brook Farm.

D 27 Dana, Gorham. "Brook Farm," _Technology Review_, 58 (January 1956): 141–143, 158–162, 164, 166–168.

General history of the community; illustrated.

D 28 Diebitsch, Roberta Watterson. "Brook Farm," in her _Some Unpublished Writings_, pp. 33–51. New Haven: Privately printed, 1939.

General, uninformative account of the community.

D 29 Doon, John Anthony, Jr. "Transcendentalism and Labor Reform." M.A. thesis, Clark University, 1959.

General account of the Brook Farmers' attitude toward labor. There were two schools of thought on labor reform that existed among the Transcendentalists. The first, led by Emerson, held that "any labor reform outside of the self reformation of the individual laborer" was evil insofar as it was "an offense against the individuality of man." The second school, led by Ripley and Bronson Alcott, held that "an active reformation of the existing society was good and that organizations which worked for the betterment of living conditions . . . were very beneficial to mankind" (pp. 18–27).

D 30 Drake, Francis S. _The Town of Roxbury_. Roxbury: Francis S. Drake, 1878.

Brief description of the community, drawing heavily on Hawthorne's writings, and the subsequent history of the land and buildings (pp. 455–460).

D 31 F. "Brook Farm, Formerly the Communists' Home," _Dorchester News_, ca. August 1875.

Description of the current state of the land and buildings at West Roxbury. Reprinted in Kenneth Walter Cameron, _Transcendental Log_ (Hartford: Transcendental Books, 1973), pp. 283–284.

D 32 Francis, Richard. "The Ideology of Brook Farm," _Studies in the American Renaissance 1977_, ed. Joel Myerson, pp. 1–48. Boston: Twayne, 1978.

Fourier's plans for labor organization and his analysis of human identity were similar to those held by the Transcendentalists. Both felt that a "simple accumulation of diverse activity frees the individual from a fixed and arbitrary social function, and enables him to become more nearly a whole person." One person who bridged the Fourierist and Transcendental philosophies was William Henry Channing, whose writings are here studied in detail. Illustrated.

D 33 Gafford, Lucile. "Transcendentalist Attitudes Toward Drama and the Theatre," New England Quarterly, 13 (September 1940): 442-466.

There were only "slight" contacts between the Brook Farmers and the theatre, although many plays were read at the community and drama was well-covered by the Harbinger (443-446, 451-457).

D 34 Gidez, Richard B. "Eden in Massachusetts: A History of Brook Farm." M.A. thesis, Columbia University, 1953. 100 pp.

General history of the community, with special attention paid to its religious aspects.

D 35 Girard, William. "De Transcendentalisme Considere Sous Son Aspect Social," University of California Publications in Modern Philology, 8 (6 August 1918): 153-226. [French]

General account of Brook Farm (166-176).

D 36 Going, Maud. "Brook Farm," McGill University Magazine, 3 (April 1904): 129-140.

General, unimportant account of the community.

D 37 Goldstein, Jonah. "Brook Farm," in his "Community and Vocation in America," pp. 36-117. Ph.D. dissertation, University of Chicago, 1971.

Brook Farm was an attempt to re-establish Puritan ideals in first a Transcendentalist and then a Fourierist setting. Among these values were man's sense of a definite role in an established social hierarchy, an affirmation of individual autonomy strengthened in service to society, and a belief in community itself.

D 38 Goodman, Ellen. "This celebrated commune has fallen on hard times," Boston Sunday Globe, 7 May 1972, pp. A-8, A-18.

Description of the present condition of the land and buildings at Brook Farm.

D 39 Greer, Louise. Browning and America. Chapel Hill: University of North Carolina Press, 1952.

Discusses the favorable reception of Robert Browning's works by the Brook Farmers (pp. 15-16).

D 40 Griscom, Stewart. "New Discoveries About Brook Farm," Boston Herald, 31 January 1937, Section B, p. 4.

Summarizes Haraszti's article in More Books (D 42).

D 41 Haney, John Louis. The Story of Our Literature. New York: Scribners, 1923.

Brook Farm was "a pleasant Utopian experience for which this queer old world was not altogether prepared"(pp. 76-77).

D 42 Haraszti, Zoltán. "Brook Farm Letters," More Books, 12 (February, March 1937): 49-68, 93-114.

An essential article, drawing upon the John Sullivan Dwight Collection at the Boston Public Library, this study presents a well-written brief survey of the community, illustrated by extensive selections from previously unpublished manuscript letters.

D 43 Haraszti, Zoltán. The Idyll of Brook Farm as Revealed by Unpublished Letters in the Boston Public Library. Boston: Trustees of the Public Library, 1937.

Reprinted from the February and March More Books; illustrations. A second, enlarged edition was published in 1940, adding a letter by Fuller written at Brook Farm and an index.

D 44 Harris, Lilian I. "Brook Farm," Inland Printer, 41 (September 1908): 883-888.

General history of the community and description of the present state of the land and buildings; illustrated.

D 45 Harris, Lilian I. "Brook Farm as it is Today," Lamp, 28 (February 1904): 7-12.

Description of the land and buildings as they were in 1904; illustrated.

D 46 Hillquit, Morris. History of Socialism in the United States. New York: Funk & Wagnalls, 1903.

General account of the community during its Fourierist period, showing that "the Brook Farmers, consciously or unconsciously, showed a decided leaning toward Fourierism from the start, and that their subsequent formal reorganization as a Phalanx was an easy and logical development, rather than a sudden conversion" (pp. 104-110).

D 47 "IV. The Brook Farm Experiment," in Selected Writings of the American Transcendentalists, ed. George Hochfield, pp. 371-396. New York: New American Library, 1966.

Reprints Ripley's correspondence with Emerson about joining Brook Farm, along with other letters by Ripley on the community, from Frothingham, George Ripley (A 112); selections from Elizabeth Peabody, "Plan of the West Roxbury Community" (B 62); and the "Introductory Statement" to the second edition of the Brook Farm Constitution (A 13).

D 48 Holloway, Mark. Heavens on Earth: Utopian Communities in America 1680–1880. London: Turnstile Press, 1951.

The introduction of Fourierism to Brook Farm had "deplorable" results (pp. 128–131, 152–154).

D 49 Johnson, Jane Maloney. "Moral Life at Brook Farm," in her "'Through Change and Through Storm': A Study of Federalist–Unitarian Thought, 1800–1860," pp. 217–286. Ph.D. dissertation, Radcliffe College, 1958.

The experiment at Brook Farm, which "bore no practical fruit," shows the decline from the earlier high morality of Unitarian thought. Hawthorne's criticism of the community's "idealistic monomania" and "soft moral idealism" in The Blithedale Romance is to the point, as is his "acid opinion" that it was the Brook Farmers' "selfishness and cowardice, thinly disguised as sensibility, which made them weak and ineffectual."

D 50 Jones, John Dillon. "A Biographical Dictionary of Brook Farm." M.A. thesis, Washington University, 1949. 117 pp.

Valuable reference work on the community and its members and visitors, drawn from published sources through 1949.

D 51 Kelley, Edythe Loretto. "Brook Farm as a Social Experiment." M.A. thesis, Washington University, 1949.

General, unimportant history of the community.

D 52 Kromer, Helen, comp. Communes and Communitarians in America. New York: Grossman Publishers, 1972.

A packet of facsimile reproductions of materials dealing with American communities, including the 14 March 1846 Harbinger describing the fire at the Phalanstery, portraits of Hawthorne, George William Curtis, Charles A. Dana, Ripley, and Horace Greeley, and a drawing of a "Plan of a Phalanstery" from the 6 June 1846 Harbinger.

D 53 Lauderbaugh, Stanley J. "Brook Farm," in his "Transcendental Utopian Experiments," pp. 31–50. M.A. thesis, Bemidji State College, 1971.

Brook Farm was closer in its early years to "uniting the laborer and the intellectual" than it was in its later years to producing "a workable solution to the problem of industrialization."

D 54 Lindell, Mildred Helene. "The Evolution of Brook Farm." M.A. thesis, University of Washington, 1931. 48 pp.

General, uninformative account of the community.

D 55 McDonald, John Alfred. "Brook Farm: A Critical Analysis of an Experiment in Utopian Socialism." M.A. thesis, Boston College, 1958. 75 pp.

An economic examination of the community shows that it was socialistic only in the most general sense, and that individualism was preserved.

D 56 McGinley, A.A. "Brook Farm To-Day," Catholic World, 61 (April 1895): 14-25.

General history of the community and description of the present condition of the land and buildings; illustrated.

D 57 Mackintosh, Charles G. Some Recollections of the Pastors and People of the Second Church of Old Roxbury. Salem: Newcomb & Gauss, 1901.

Lists the various owners of Brook Farm since 1825 (pp. 70-72).

D 58 MacNab, John E. "Unitarians and Socialistic Ideas in the United States Prior to 1860," Proceedings of the Unitarian Historical Society, 10 (1953): 3-27.

General account of the Unitarians at or connected with Brook Farm.

D 59 Menzi, Marjorie Jean. "Women's Rights: An Aspect of Transcendentalism as Exhibited by Brook Farm." M.A. thesis, Columbia University, 1967. 127 pp.

Brook Farm favorably applied the Transcendental doctrines of "freedom from restraints; undesirability of conformity; self-reliance; self-culture; individualism; and equality resulting from similar access to the Divine through nature" to woman's position in life.

D 60 Mitchell, Anna M. "The Brook Farm Movement Viewed through the Perspective of Half a Century," Catholic World, 73 (April 1901): 17-31.

General account of the community and its major participants; illustrated.

D 61   Mitchell, Donald G. American Lands and Letters: Leather-
       Stocking to Poe's "Raven". New York: Scribners, 1899.

       General history of Brook Farm (pp. 156-169); illustrated.

D 62   Muncy, Raymond Lee. Sex and Marriage in Utopian Communities:
       19th-Century America. Bloomington: Indiana University
       Press, 1973.

       General discussion of the attitudes toward sex and
       marriage at Brook Farm, which of all the Fourierist
       communities was the least gossiped about (pp. 79-88).

D 63   Myerson, Joel. "An Ungathered Sanborn Lecture on Brook
       Farm," American Transcendental Quarterly, No. 26 (Spring
       1975): Supplement 1-11.

       General history of the community with Sanborn's
       comments on the participants. Reprinted as
       "Reminiscences of Brook Farm and its Founders," in
       Sanborn, Transcendental and Literary New England, ed.
       Kenneth Walter Cameron (Hartford: Transcendental Books,
       1975), pp. 230-239.

D 64   Nelson, Truman. The Passion by the Brook. Garden City,
       N.Y.: Doubleday, 1953.

       A novel based on Brook Farm which manages to obscure the
       author's genuine knowledge of the period with an overly
       sentimentalized portrait of the community.

       Reviews:

       Kirkus, 21 (1 January 1953): 18-19. This book is
           seriously marred by the author's "ill-disguised
           cynicism and tongue in cheek attitude towards the
           falsities of the motives" which contributed to the
           "conception and decay" of Brook Farm.
       Byam, Milton S. Library Journal, 78 (15 February 1953):
           375. This is a "dull" book with "flat" characters.
       Harding, Walter. "Brook Farm Again: A Vivid Panorama of
           that 'Utopia,'" Magazine of Books [Chicago Tribune],
           8 March 1953, p. 4. Nelson's characters are "alive,"
           though his totally fictional love triangle rings false.
       Nerber, John. "Disillusion in Utopia," New York Times
           Book Review, 8 March 1953, p. 27. Nelson has
           "succeeded in capturing Brook Farm as it pretty much
           must have been."
       [Hughes, Riley.] Catholic World, 177 (April 1953): 73-74.
           This book distorts the Fourierist period of Brook Farm
           and puts too much emphasis on the sensual.
       Rugoff, Milton. "New England Conscience," New York
           Herald Tribune Book Review, 5 April 1953, p. 10. As

an "historical interpretation" of Brook Farm, this
book is "bold and shrewd"; as fiction, it is
"delightful."

Brooks, Tom. "Too Little Farming," New Republic, 128
(13 April 1953): 23. Nelson has produced a pleasant
book, though his writing is "often awkward."

Cannon, Lee E. "The Treason of the Heart," Christian
Century, 70 (7 October 1953): 1135. Nelson has
written a "fascinating" history of Brook Farm.

D 65 Nissenbaum, Stephen. "Transcendentalism: From Parish to
Church." M.A. thesis, Columbia University, 1963.

General study of Brook Farm's relations with Unitarian
pastoral theology, Fourierism, and Catholicism (pp.
40-79).

D 66 Noyes, John Humphrey. History of American Socialisms.
Philadelphia: Lippincott, 1870.

During its early period, Brook Farm was mainly influenced
by the "religious Socialism" of William Henry Channing.
Its later period was influenced by Fourierism and
Swedenborgianism. Noyes' account is drawn mainly from
published contemporary documents (pp. 102-118, 512-563).

D 67 Pax, Joseph M. "Saints of New England," Nuntius Aulae [St.
Charles Seminary, Carthagena, Ohio], 27 (July 1944):
119-129.

General account of Brook Farm, concentrating on the
contacts with Catholicism by its members. Reprinted in
an abridged form in Catholic Digest, 8 (August 1944):
80-85.

D 68 Putnam, Hannah S. "The Development of Brook Farm as an
Experiment in Social Reconstruction." Undergraduate
honors thesis, Smith College, 1942. 49 pp.

Brook Farm failed because, in a period of industrial-
ization, "a self-sufficient community was unsound."
Also, the general public reaction against socialism and
Fourierism drew away possible support.

D 69 Reilly, Rev. Francis A. "Brook Farm." M.A. thesis, St.
Bonaventure University, 1944.

Not seen; library's copy unlocated.

D 70 Rodgers, Ada S. "The Influence of Fourierism Upon
Transcendental Efforts of Group Living at Brook Farm."
M.A. thesis, University of Texas at El Paso, 1969.
28 pp.

The introduction of Fourierism "undermined" the
community's chances for success.

D 71 Roxbury, Mass. Joint Special Committee. <u>Report of the
Joint Special Committee on the Buildings at Brook Farm,
and a New Almshouse</u>. Roxbury: Joseph G. Torrey, 1849.

The Committee reports that the existing buildings at
Brook Farm are too spread out for the central control
needed for the inmates of the almshouse, and recommends
constructing a new, single large structure for this
purpose.

D 72 Roxbury, Mass. Joint Special Committee. <u>Report of the
Joint Special Committee on the Removal of the Alms House,
and the Purchase of "Brook Farm"</u>. Roxbury: Joseph G.
Torrey, 1849.

Brook Farm and its buildings should be purchased by the
city of Roxbury and the almshouse moved there. The land
was purchased at auction on 13 April 1849 for $19,150.

D 73 Ryll, Charlyn Tye. "Fourier and the Farmers: The Influence
of Fourierism on the Reorganization of Brook Farm." M.A.
thesis, University of Virginia, 1969. 78 pp.

The most serious defects of Brook Farm were Ripley's
"naive beliefs concerning human nature and social
organization," and the "sterile completeness of Fourier's
system."

D 74 <u>Autobiography of Brook Farm</u>, ed. Henry W. Sams. Englewood
Cliffs, N.J.: Prentice-Hall, 1958.

Excellent anthology tracing the historical development
of Brook Farm. Chapters deal with "From the Beginning
to the Earliest Articles of Association: 1840-1841,"
"From Association to Phalanx: 1841-1844," "From Phalanx
to the Fire: 1844-1846," "The Last Days: 1846-1847," and
"Brook Farm Remembered: 1847-1928." Selections are
printed from manuscript letters: in the Elijah P. Grant
Papers at the University of Chicago; from Hawthorne to
Louisa Hawthorne of 3 May 1841, and to Sophia Peabody of
13 April, 1 June, 12 August, 22 August, 3 September, 22
September, 25 September, and 29 September 1841 at the
Henry E. Huntington Library; and by various members of
the community written between 1843 and 1847 at the
Middlebury College Library (see G 213, G 219, G 220,
G 225). Selections are reprinted from: "The Rev. George
Ripley," <u>Monthly Miscellany</u> (A 106); "The Community at
West Roxbury, Mass.," <u>Monthly Miscellany</u> (B 1); Peabody,
"Plan of the West Roxbury Community" (B 62); articles in
the <u>Phalanx</u> (1843-1845); Lane, "American Correspondence"
(B 58); Brook Farm, <u>Constitution</u> (1st ed., B 12); Dana,

A Lecture on Association . . . with Religion (A 36);
Dwight, A Lecture on Association . . . with Education
(A 42); Brook Farm, Constitution (2nd ed., B 13); Lane,
"Brook Farm" (B 59); articles in the Harbinger (1845-
1846); Memoirs of Margaret Fuller Ossoli (B 40);
Hawthorne, The Blithedale Romance (A 52); Russell, "Home
Life of the Brook Farm Association" (A 129); Dwight,
"Music a Means of Culture" (A 43); Frothingham, George
Ripley (A 112); Emerson, "Historic Notes of Life and
Letters in Massachusetts" (B 23); Higginson, Margaret
Fuller Ossoli (B 41); Kirby, Years of Experience (A 96);
Codman, Brook Farm (A 22); Sumner, "A Boy's Recollections
of Brook Farm" (A 136); Cooke, John Sullivan Dwight (A 44);
Curtis, Early Letters (A 25); Swift, Brook Farm (D 82);
Sedgwick, "A Girl of Sixteen at Brook Farm" (A 134);
Emerson, Journals (B 24, 1909-1914 ed.); Sears, My Friends
at Brook Farm (A 133); Dwight, Letters from Brook Farm
(A 48); Hawthorne, American Notebooks (A 50); Haraszti,
The Idyll of Brook Farm (D 43, 1937 ed.); Alcott, Journals
(B 2); Emerson, Letters (B 25); Hawthorne, "Hawthorne and
Utopian Socialism" (A 72); and letters from Isaac Hecker
in The Correspondence of Henry David Thoreau, ed. Walter
Harding and Carl Bode (Washington Square: New York
University Press, 1957).

D 75   Sams, Henry W. Teacher's Manual. Autobiography of Brook
       Farm. Englewood Cliffs, N.J.: Prentice-Hall, 1958.
       18 pp.

       Contains a number of good "Suggestions to Teachers."

D 76   [Sanborn, F.B.] "Our Boston Literary Letter. Thoreau,
       Newcomb, Brook Farm," Springfield Republican, 2 December
       1896, p. 5.

       General comments on Kirby's Years of Experience (A 96),
       Charles King Newcomb, and Elliott's Life of Father Hecker
       (A 88).

D 77   Sceery, Edwin James. Transcendentalism: A Story of Brook
       Farm. Boston: Meador, 1940.

       Brief, uninformative account of the community, originally
       written as a research paper at the Teachers College of
       Connecticut.

D 78   Smart, George K. "A New England Adventure in Idealism,"
       Travel, 74 (November 1939): 14-15, 39.

       General account of Brook Farm; illustrated.

D 79   Spencer, Benjamin T. The Quest for Nationality: An American
       Literary Campaign. Syracuse: Syracuse University Press,
       1957.

The Brook Farmers cared for an American national
literature only when it was indicative of a more
universal spirit, promoting "the solution of problems
which agitate the soul" (pp. 176-177).

D 80 Stoehr, Taylor. "Transcendentalist Attitudes Toward
Communitism and Individualism," ESQ: A Journal of the
American Renaissance, 20 (II Quarter 1974): 65-90.

Surveys attitudes towards Brook Farm, Fruitlands, and
the Shakers held by the major Transcendentalists.

D 81 Swift, Lindsay. "Brook Farm," Current Literature, 28
(April 1900): 70-73.

Reprinted from Swift, Brook Farm.

D 82 Swift, Lindsay. Brook Farm: Its Members, Scholars, and
Visitors. New York: Macmillan, 1900.

Swift's book is still the best history of Brook Farm
available. He has organized his study by topics
("Organization," "Buildings and Grounds," "Industries,"
"Household Work," "Amusements and Customs," "The School
and Its Scholars," "Members," "Visitors," "The Harbinger,"
and "Albert Brisbane and Fourierism") and has drawn
heavily and with discretion from previously published
recollections and histories to present his well-written
and balanced account of the community. Also included is
the first printing of a letter from Georgiana Bruce during
the summer of 1842 describing daily life at Brook Farm.
An essential work for anyone writing on Brook Farm.

Reviews:

"The Story of Brook Farm," Boston Evening Transcript,
24 January 1900, p. 6. This "loving and thorough
labor" is an excellent history of the community.
[Chadwick, John White.] Nation, 70 (22 February 1900):
152. "Mr. Swift has done his work so well that the
task seems to have waited for his coming, and there
can be no good excuse for any one's taking it up again
hereafter."
"Current Literature," Boston Herald, 24 March 1900, p. 8.
Swift's book gains perspective by his somewhat
skeptical attitude towards the experiment.
"Brook Farm," Book Buyer, 20 (April 1900): 240-241. This
book is "scholarly, unpretentious, [and] readable."
[Sanborn, F.B.] "Our Boston Literary Letter," Springfield
Republican, 27 April 1900. Swift's book suffers from
its author's attitude of superiority towards many of
his subjects, especially Bronson Alcott.
"A Famous Experiment," Academy, 58 (16 June 1900): 516-517.
Swift has written a good account of a noble experiment.

T[raubel, Horace.] "Brook Farm," *Conservator*, 11 (July 1900): 76. This is an excellent account of an experiment whose ideals are uplifting for all men.

D 83 T., C.B. "Brook Farm as It Is," New York *Evening Post*, 14 December 1881, p. 3.

Description of the present state of the buildings and grounds.

D 84 Tarbell, Arthur W. "The Brook Farm Experiment," *National Magazine*, 7 (December 1897): 195–203.

General account of the community; illustrated with original drawings by Walter L. Greene.

D 85 Titus, Eunice E. "The Influence that Produced Brook Farm." M.A. thesis, Columbia University, 1913. 36 pp.

General, uninformative account of the community.

D 86 Trent, William P. *A History of American Literature 1607–1865*. New York: Appleton, 1903.

Somewhat skeptical account of Brook Farm, concluding that at present it brings to mind "poetical ploughmen and philosophical milkers" rather than any "more specifically spiritual and literary features" (pp. 306–309).

D 87 Tyler, Alice Felt. *Freedom's Ferment*. Minneapolis: University of Minnesota Press, 1944.

General history of Brook Farm (pp. 175–184).

D 88 Wallster, Jeanne A. "'Ripley's Farm': Brook Farm Reinterpreted." M.A. thesis, Boston College, 1966. 94 pp.

Brook Farm was part of the "indigenous American communitarian tradition," and cannot be classified as either completely Transcendental or Fourierist.

D 89 Webber, Everett. *Escape to Utopia: The Communal Movement in America*. New York: Hastings House, 1959.

General account of the community, including the first printing of a letter of 25 July 1843 by Sophia Eastman about daily life at Brook Farm (see G 213; pp. 170–192).

D 90 Wendell, Barrett. *A Literary History of America*. New York: Scribners, 1900.

Brook Farm was typical of all Transcendentalism: it "had a bright beginning, a rather bewildering adolescence, and a confused, misty end; but it left no one the worse for its influence" (pp. 305-309).

D 91 Wilson, J.B. "The Antecedents of Brook Farm," New England Quarterly, 15 (June 1942): 320-331.

The educational efforts of Josiah Holbrook's Agricultural Seminary (later the American Lyceum), and of the Pestalozzian or Infant-School Society greatly influenced teaching concepts at Brook Farm.

D 92 Wilson, John B. "Brook Farm: Seedbed of Education," School and Society, 94 (22 January 1966): 43-47.

General description of the educational experiments at the community.

D 93 Wilson, Rufus Rockwell. New England in Letters. New York: A. Wessels, 1904.

General account of Brook Farm (pp. 268-276).

D 94 Wolfe, Theodore F. Literary Shrines. Philadelphia: Lippincott, 1895.

Brief description of the present state of the land and buildings at Brook Farm (pp. 147-151).

D 95 Worthley, Evans A. "Brook Farm Might Succeed Today," Christian Leader, 27 February, 6 March 1937, pp. 272-274, 307-308.

A comparison of Brook Farm with the Amana Colony in Iowa shows that had Ripley been able to spread the community's indebtedness over a long period of time, and had he obtained fire insurance on the Phalanstery, the community would have succeeded.

D 96 Zolla, Elémire. Le Origini del Transcendentalismo. Rome: Edizioni di Storia e Letteratura, 1963. [Italian]

General account of Brook Farm (pp. 235-240).

SECTION E: THE HARBINGER

THE HARBINGER

THE HARBINGER

E 1 The Harbinger published eight volumes between 14 June 1845 and 10 February 1849. Volumes one through four were published by the Brook Farm Phalanx, volume five by the American Union of Associationists in Boston, and volumes six through eight by the American Union of Associationists in New York. The first five volumes were edited and published at Brook Farm, the remainder, after the collapse of the community, by various ex-Brook Farmers in New York. Unfortunately for students of the history of Brook Farm, the Harbinger was more interested in promoting associationism than in promoting Brook Farm, and articles on the community itself are scarce. Of the many articles on associationism, perhaps the best brief statement is Albert Brisbane, "The American Associationists," 2 (7 March 1846): 200–203.

E 2 "To the Friends of the Harbinger," Harbinger, 3 (13 June 1846): 12.

Notice that the Harbinger is in need of more paid subscriptions in order to continue. The request drew immediate support; see "Correspondence," 3 (20 June 1846): 17–18.

E 3 Cooke, George Willis. An Historical and Biographical Introduction to Accompany THE DIAL. 2 vols. Cleveland: Rowfant Club, 1902.

General comments on Brook Farm throughout both volumes. The Harbinger is discussed as a successor to the Dial (1:184–189).

E 4 Delano, Sterling F. "The Harbinger: A Portrait of Associationism in America." Ph.D. dissertation, Southern Illinois University, 1973. 213 pp.

Despite its Fourierist bias, the Harbinger was eclectic in its interests. Chapters discuss the history of the Harbinger, its connection with associationism, its treatment of social, political, and economic matters, and its literary criticism.

E 5   Frothingham, Octavius Brooks. <u>Transcendentalism in New England</u>. New York: Putnams, 1876.

General history of Brook Farm and the <u>Harbinger</u> (pp. 157-175, 325-332).

E 6   Gallant, Barbara Gans. "George Ripley and <u>The Harbinger</u>," in her "The New England Transcendentalists and the European Revolutions of 1848," pp. 83-93. M.A. thesis, University of Florida, 1966.

Ripley and the <u>Harbinger</u> remained supportive towards the French Revolution, though on occasions the violence of the movement caused their comments to be a mixture of "disappointment and hope."

E 7   Gohdes, Clarence L.F. "<u>The Harbinger</u>," in his <u>The Periodicals of American Transcendentalism</u>, pp. 101-131. Durham: Duke University Press, 1931.

Valuable account of the Brook Farm periodical, which successfully confronted the problem of "producing a more or less literary paper which might advance the cause of Fourierism."

E 8   Jones, Howard Mumford. "American Comment on George Sand, 1837-1848," <u>American Literature</u>, 3 (January 1932): 389-407.

It is "at least doubtful whether <u>The Harbinger</u> support [of Sand] was not as damaging as it was helpful" (405-406).

E 9   Joyaux, Georges Jules. "French Thought in American Magazines 1800-1848." Ph.D. dissertation, Michigan State University, 1951.

Annotated listing of the <u>Harbinger</u>'s comments on French writers from 1845 to 1847 (pp. 563-565, 581-583, 599-601).

E 10 Joyaux, Georges J. "George Sand, Eugène Sue, and <u>The Harbinger</u>," <u>French Review</u>, 27 (December 1953): 122-131.

The <u>Harbinger</u> defended Sand against charges of immorality and of being favorable towards Fourierism, and translated two of her novels for serial publication. Sue's appeal to the <u>Harbinger</u> was his espousal of Fourierist principles. In general, the <u>Harbinger</u> considered social thought more important than literary talent.

E 11   Kaufman, Marjorie Ruth. "The Literary Reviews of the
       Harbinger During its Brook Farm Period 1845-1847." M.A.
       thesis, University of Washington, 1947. 134 pp.

   Between June 1845 and June 1847 the literary reviews of
   the Harbinger, especially those written by Charles A.
   Dana, Dwight, and Ripley, were characterized by: an
   "optimistic idealism"; the belief that social problems
   all had a solution; a desire that literature should
   contain constructive social criticism; and a view of the
   artist as "the prophet of a better life."

E 12   Lowens, Irving. "Writings about Music in the Periodicals
       of American Transcendentalism (1835-1850)," Journal of
       the American Musicological Society, 10 (Summer 1957):
       71-85.

   The Harbinger was "far and away the most important
   medium through which Transcendental-colored ideas about
   music were disseminated." All but twenty-six of the 183
   articles on music listed in an appendix are from the
   Brook Farm paper.

E 13   Mott, Frank Luther. "The Harbinger," in his A History of
       American Magazines 1741-1850, pp. 763-765. New York:
       Appleton, 1930.

   Brief account of the Brook Farm paper.

E 14   Powell, Janette C. "A Study of the Harbinger." M.A. thesis,
       University of Chicago, 1925. 49 pp.

   General treatment of the Brook Farm paper and its
   support of associationism.

E 15   Rabinovitz, Albert L. "Criticism of French Novels in Boston
       Magazines, 1830-1860," New England Quarterly, 14
       (September 1941): 488-504.

   The Harbinger was George Sand's "steady defender" in
   New England. Eugène Sue's favorable view of Fourierism
   assured him of a positive reception from the paper
   (495-496, 498-499).

E 16   [Ripley, George.] "The Harbinger," Phalanx, 1 (3 May 1845):
       340.

   Prospectus of the new paper to be published at Brook
   Farm.

E 17   [Ripley, George.] "Introductory Notice," Harbinger, 1 (14
       June 1845): 8-10.

   General statement of aims and goals.

E 18 Vogel, Stanley M. <u>German Literary Influences on the American Transcendentalists</u>. New Haven: Yale University Press, 1955.

    Describes the influence of German literature on the Brook Farmers and especially the <u>Harbinger</u>, in which "almost every phase of German literature was canvassed" (pp. 76-78).

SECTION F: ANA

ANA

F 1   Brook Farm: The Amusing and Memorable of American Country Life. New York: Robert Carter, 1860.

   Novel; not about Ripley's community.

F 2   Cushman, Herbert Ernest. "Summer Brook Farm," Outlook, 57 (13 November 1897): 665-667.

   Brief account of a community in the Adirondacks named after the one at West Roxbury; nothing on Brook Farm.

F 3   Gordon, George Henry. Brook Farm to Cedar Mountain. Boston: James R. Osgood, 1883.

   Deals with the army's use of the land and buildings at Brook Farm during the Civil War; no information about Ripley's community.

F 4   [Guiney, Louise Imogen.] "Brook Farm," Harper's New Monthly Magazine, 69 (September 1884): 628.

   Poem.

F 5   Holbrook, Stewart H. "Brook Farm, Wild West Style," American Mercury, 57 (August 1943): 216-223.

   Account of a community at Home, Washington; no significant references to Brook Farm.

F 6   [Mullan, William.] Furrows Through Brook Farm. Boston: William Mullan, 1899.

   Poem.

   Reviews:

   "Brook Farm," Boston Evening Transcript, 11 April 1900, p. 13. This book is marked by a "pedestrian" muse which "keeps to the middle of the road" and "does not seem to have secured just the right point of view."

SECTION G: MANUSCRIPTS

MANUSCRIPTS

BOSTON PUBLIC LIBRARY

The John Sullivan Dwight Collection at the Boston Public Library
is a letterbook containing nearly 100 letters by and to Dwight,
many relating to Brook Farm. The library owns a negative microfilm
of the collection from which a positive microfilm may be made at a
nominal cost. Many of the Brook Farm letters are printed in
Haraszti, The Idyll of Brook Farm (D 43).

G 1   George Ripley to Dwight, West Roxbury, 7 July 1840,
      Ms.E.4.1.(24).

      Ripley comments about his resignation from the Purchase
      Street church, and on the first number of the Dial.

G 2   Sophia Ripley to Dwight, [West Roxbury], 1 August 1840,
      Ms.E.4.1.(26).

      A description of the farm the Ripleys have settled at
      in West Roxbury. Quoted in The Idyll of Brook Farm,
      pp. 12-13.

G 3   George Ripley to Dwight, Brook Farm, 6 August 1840,
      Ms.E.4.1.(27).

      Ripley is glad that the publication of the Dial has
      caused such a great stir in the press.

G 4   Elizabeth Peabody to Dwight, Boston, 20 September 1840,
      Ms.E.4.1.(28).

      Peabody informs Dwight about some recent Transcendental
      Club meetings.

G 5   Samuel Osgood to Dwight, Nashua, New Hampshire, 21 November
      1840. Ms.E.4.1.(29).

      Osgood saw Ripley in Boston and is excited by the plans
      for the proposed community. Quoted in The Idyll of Brook
      Farm, p. 14.

G 6 Elizabeth Peabody to Dwight, [Boston], [26 April 1841].
    Ms.E.4.1.(33).

    Peabody tells about the first arrivals at Brook Farm,
    including Hawthorne. There will be a meeting at her
    house on 12 May to discuss the future of the community,
    especially the school, and to raise money. Quoted in
    The Idyll of Brook Farm, pp. 14-17.

G 7 Sophia Ripley to Dwight, Boston, 6 May [1841].
    Ms.E.4.1.(34).

    There are now sixteen people at Brook Farm. Daily
    activities are described. Quoted in The Idyll of
    Brook Farm, pp. 17-18.

G 8 Elizabeth Peabody to Dwight, [Boston], 24 June 1841.
    Ms.E.4.1.(35).

    Peabody fears Brook Farm will not come of age unless
    Ripley is more active in publicizing it. Quoted in
    The Idyll of Brook Farm, pp. 18-19.

G 9 Dwight to Reverend James Flint, Brook Farm, 18 June 1842.
    Ms.E.4.1.(37).

    Dwight has decided to quit preaching as a profession.

G 10 Lydia Maria Child to Dwight, New York, 1 December 1842.
    Ms.E.4.1.(40).

    Child asks about sending a recent widow, Caroline
    Henshaw Colt, to Brook Farm. (She was not admitted.)
    Quoted, with details about Mrs. Colt, in The Idyll of
    Brook Farm, pp. 22-25.

G 11 George William Curtis to Dwight, New York, 11 November 1843.
    Ms.E.4.1.(46).

    Curtis already misses the people and culture at Brook
    Farm.

G 12 Samuel Longfellow to Dwight, Horta, Fayal, the Azores, 19
    February 1844. Ms.E.4.1.(47).

    Longfellow inquires about the membership rules and
    possibilities for schooling at Brook Farm. Quoted in
    The Idyll of Brook Farm, p. 26.

G 13 Christopher List to Dwight, Philadelphia, 14 March 1845.
    Ms.E.4.1.(49).

    List has read Dwight's letter to James Kay about the
    reorganization of Brook Farm along Fourierist lines

and says he is fully in support of it. Quoted in The
Idyll of Brook Farm, pp. 33-34.

G 14 Samuel Osgood to Dwight, Providence, 1 July 1845.
Ms.E.4.1.(50).

Osgood renews his subscription to the Harbinger and
wishes the community well. Quoted in The Idyll of
Brook Farm, p. 34.

G 15 Albert Brisbane to Dwight, New York, 2 December 1845.
Ms.E.4.1.(52).

Brisbane comments on the progress of associationism.
Quoted in The Idyll of Brook Farm, p. 31.

G 16 Albert Brisbane to Dwight, New York, [15 December 1845].
Ms.E.4.1.(53).

Brisbane comments on the progress of associationism.

G 17 Albert Brisbane to Dwight, New York, 30 December 1845.
Ms.E.4.1.(54).

Brisbane comments on the progress of associationism.
Quoted in The Idyll of Brook Farm, pp. 31-32.

G 18 William Henry Channing to Dwight, Brattleboro, Vermont,
18 January 1846. Ms.E.4.1.(55).

Even if Brook Farm should fail, Channing feels the
cause of unity will remain to unite people in a single
reform movement. Quoted in The Idyll of Brook Farm,
pp. 34-35.

G 19 Georgiana Bruce to Dwight, Alton, Illinois, 18 January 1846.
Ms.E.4.1.(56).

Bruce misses Brook Farm but keeps up on it by reading
the Harbinger. She has obtained seven new subscriptions
for the paper in Illinois.

G 20 Charles Dana to Dwight, [Brook Farm?], [March 1846].
Ms.E.4.1.(57).

The Brook Farmers will meet with the creditors and
holders of loans on the community to ask for a reduction
in their interest rates. If this is not possible, then
they will have to declare bankruptcy. Quoted in The
Idyll of Brook Farm, pp. 38-41.

G 21 James Kay to Dwight, Philadelphia, 2 March 1846.
Ms.E.4.1.(58).

Kay despairs more than ever about the possibilities
for the success of Brook Farm. There has been too much
emphasis on associationism and reform, and not enough on
making each member working to make the community pay its
own way. Quoted in The Idyll of Brook Farm, pp. 36-37.

G 22 Sophia Ripley to Dwight, [Brook Farm?], 14 March [1846].
Ms.E.4.1.(59).

Everyone at Brook Farm has read with interest his
letter about life in New York. They have reviewed
their financial accounts and have almost decided to
give up all their property and start anew. Quoted in
The Idyll of Brook Farm, pp. 37-38.

G 23 Dwight to George Ripley, New York, 16 March 1846.
Ms.E.4.1.(60).

Dwight has been lecturing on associationism. He has
talked to Horace Greeley, Marcus Spring, and others,
who have agreed to give up their stocks in Brook Farm
and even buy new shares to help continue the community.
Ripley may consider all stock in Brook Farm held in New
York as cancelled.

G 24 George Ripley to Dwight, Brook Farm, 19 March 1846.
Ms.E.4.1.(61).

Ripley describes the future prospects of the community
after the Phalanstery fire. He also comments on the
belated celebration of Charles A. Dana's marriage.
Quoted in The Idyll of Brook Farm, p. 38.

G 25 Edward Tweedy to Dwight, New York, 18 April 1846.
Ms.E.4.1.(62).

Tweedy wishes Brook Farm well and says a Dr. Wilkenson
would have no objection to seeing his favorable letter
on the community published in the Harbinger.

G 26 James Kay to Dwight, Philadelphia, 22 April 1846.
Ms.E.4.1.(63).

Kay sends money to pay for his board during a recent
visit to Brook Farm. He will try to raise money for
the community in Philadelphia. Quoted in The Idyll of
Brook Farm, pp. 41-42.

G 27 Marcus Spring to Dwight, Uxbridge, New York, 29 May 1846.
Ms.E.4.1.(64).

Spring wishes to be sent current issues of the Harbinger.

G 28   William Henry Channing to Dwight, Rondout, New York, 8 November 1846. Ms.E.4.1.(65).

Channing gives his feelings about the possibilities for the future of reform. Quoted in The Idyll of Brook Farm, pp. 42-43.

G 29   John Orvis to Dwight, Middlebury, Vermont, 9 December 1846. Ms.E.4.1.(66).

Orvis sends in money for subscriptions to the Harbinger and gives an account of his recent lectures on behalf of associationism. Quoted in The Idyll of Brook Farm, pp. 44-45.

G 30   John Allen to Dwight, Cincinnati, 27 April 1848. Ms.E.4.1.(68).

Allen comments on the future of associationism.

G 31   Parke Godwin to Dwight, New York, 8 December 1848. Ms.E.4.1.(70).

Godwin complains that the literary department of the Harbinger is being neglected.

G 32   Fanny Macdaniel to Dwight, [Brook Farm], 28 April n.y. Ms.E.4.1.(91).

Macdaniel asks for information about the Brook Farm school for a friend.

KANSAS STATE HISTORICAL SOCIETY

The Microfilm Edition of the John Stillman Brown Family Papers deposited at the Kansas State Historical Society is available for purchase or interlibrary loan on positive microfilm. A printed guide to the collection is also available; see A 15.

G 33   Charles A. Dana to John S. Brown, Brook Farm, 12 January 1841. Reel One, "Correspondence and Papers, 1818-1857," frames 454-457.

Enthusiastic letter about Brook Farm's chances for success. Brown would be an instructor in theosophical and practical agriculture in the Brook Farm school during 1842.

G 34   Wing Russell to Hannah Ripley, Syracuse, New York, 26 June 1842. Reel One, "Correspondence and Papers, 1818-1857," frames 471-474.

Russell wishes her well at Brook Farm, which he thinks can succeed. He especially likes their religious toleration. Miss Ripley was Brown's sister-in-law.

G 35 Mary R. Brown to John S. Brown, Buffalo, New York, 5 July 1842. Reel One, "Correspondence and Papers, 1818–1857," frames 475–478.

Mrs. Brown is upset because Charles A. Dana has been sending letters requesting financial support for Brook Farm.

G 36 John S. Brown to Mary R. Brown, Brook Farm, 12 September 1842. Reel One, "Correspondence and Papers, 1818–1857," frames 479–482.

Brown gives a general description of Brook Farm.

G 37 Charles A. Dana to Hannah Ripley, Brook Farm, 22 September 1842. Reel One, "Correspondence and Papers, 1818–1857," frames 483–486.

Dana gives a general description of Brook Farm. He is plagued by self-doubts but hopes they will pass.

G 38 John S. Brown to Mary R. Brown, Brook Farm, [17 October 1842?]. Reel One, "Correspondence and Papers, 1818–1857," frames 491–494.

Brown describes the life at Brook Farm. He is homesick for his wife and children.

G 39 George W. Hosum to Mr. and Mrs. John S. Brown, Buffalo, 3 July 1843. Reel One, "Correspondence and Papers, 1818–1857," frames 510–513.

Hosum regrets he was unable to visit the Browns at Brook Farm during his recent trip through New England. While he was in Concord he visited Charles Lane and Bronson Alcott, and he describes their plans for Fruitlands with some skepticism.

G 40 George William Curtis to Hannah Ripley, Brook Farm, 13 July 1843. Reel One, "Correspondence and Papers, 1818–1857," frames 514–517.

Curtis comments on his friends at Brook Farm.

G 41 George Ripley to John S. Brown, Brook Farm, 6 November 1843. Reel One, "Correspondence and Papers, 1818–1857," frames 518–519.

Ripley regrets that Brown is away from the community.

G 42   Mary R. Brown to John S. Brown, Brook Farm, 20 November 1843. Reel One, "Correspondence and Papers, 1818-1857," frames 520-523.

Mrs. Brown describes her life at Brook Farm.

G 43   John S. Brown to Mary R. Brown, Brattleboro, Vermont, 26 November 1843. Reel One, "Correspondence and Papers, 1818-1857," frames 524-527.

Brown has decided to leave Brook Farm and is looking for a ministerial appointment while on his travels.

G 44   Mary R. Brown to John S. Brown, Brook Farm, 28 January 1844. Reel One, "Correspondence and Papers, 1818-1857," frames 532-535.

Mrs. Brown hopes her husband will not hastily accept a parish assignment, for she fears he will be bored by the daily chores of being a minister. She describes a visit to Brook Farm by Emerson, and reports on the community's attempts to raise money.

G 45   John S. Brown to Mary R. Brown, Hingham, Massachusetts, 10 March 1844. Reel One, "Correspondence and Papers, 1818-1857," frames 536-539.

Although Brown feels that the reorganization of Brook Farm is for the best, he still feels he cannot remain a member of the community and still provide for his family.

G 46   Charles A. Dana to Hannah Ripley, Brook Farm, 25 January [1845]. Reel One, "Correspondence and Papers, 1818-1857," frames 555-557.

Dana is busy writing lectures and "constitutions."

G 47   Charles A. Dana to Hannah Ripley, [Brook Farm], 28 April [1845]. Reel One, "Correspondence and Papers, 1818-1857," frames 562-564.

Dana accepts her offer for him to visit Hingham and lecture on "Association, or Society based upon Christianity."

G 48   Charles A. Dana to Hannah Ripley, [Brook Farm], 6 July 1845. Reel One, "Correspondence and Papers, 1818-1857," frames 565-567.

Dana does not know the authors of articles in the Harbinger, but this is unimportant, for "They are not the productions of individuals but the words of a school."

G 49 Charles A. Dana to Hannah Ripley, Brook Farm, 27 October 1845. Reel One, "Correspondence and Papers, 1818–1857," frames 568–571.

Dana feels that the Brook Farm experiment is "all over."

G 50 Charles A. Dana to Hannah Ripley, [Brook Farm], [1846?]. Reel One, "Correspondence and Papers, 1818–1857," frames 577–578.

Dana will send her the back issues of the Harbinger that she requested.

G 51 Charles A. Dana to Hannah Ripley, New York, 5 September 1847. Reel One, "Correspondence and Papers, 1818–1857," frames 593–596.

The Ripleys will soon be joining him in New York and they will all work together in furthering the cause of socialism.

MASSACHUSETTS HISTORICAL SOCIETY

The Brook Farm collection at the Massachusetts Historical Society consists of about 150 letters, five journals and day books, miscellaneous manuscript material, and miscellaneous newspaper and periodical clippings. The Society has copied the manuscript material on two reels of positive microfilm, which may be purchased for $50. Most of the letters were written from Brook Farm by Marianne Dwight (later Mrs. John Orvis) to her friend Anna Q.T. Parsons and her brother, Frank. They are full of information on the daily life of the community. The majority of Dwight's letters are printed in Letters from Brook Farm 1844–1847, ed. Amy L. Reed (A 48). Reed does not print the full text for all letters but does indicate omissions. Some letters printed by Reed are not on the microfilm. Inferred dates assigned to letters are the Society's.

ROLL ONE

G 52 Marianne Dwight to Anna Q.T. Parsons, Boston, 21 May 1843.

G 53 Marianne Dwight to Anna Q.T. Parsons, Boston, 4 July 1843.

G 54 Marianne Dwight to Anna Q.T. Parsons, Boston, 24 August 1843.

G 55   Marianne Dwight to Anna Q.T. Parsons, [Brook Farm], [September 1843?].

   Dated "[Spring 1844]" in Letters from Brook Farm, pp. 1-4.

G 56   Marianne Dwight to Anna Q.T. Parsons, [Brook Farm], [September 1843].

   Dated "[1844]" in Letters from Brook Farm, pp. 4-7.

G 57   Marianne Dwight to Anna Q.T. Parsons, Brook Farm, September 1843.

G 58   Marianne Dwight to Frank Dwight, Brook Farm, 14 April 1844.

   Letters from Brook Farm, pp. 7-10.

G 59   Marianne Dwight to Anna Q.T. Parsons, Brook Farm, 17 April 1844.

   Letters from Brook Farm, pp. 10-12.

G 60   Marianne Dwight to Anna Q.T. Parsons, Brook Farm, 27 April [1844].

   Letters from Brook Farm, pp. 12-15.

G 61   Marianne Dwight to Frank Dwight, Brook Farm, 2 May [1844].

G 62   Marianne Dwight to Anna Q.T. Parsons, Brook Farm, 11 May [1844].

   Letters from Brook Farm, pp. 15-17.

G 63   Anna Q.T. Parsons to Marianne Dwight, Boston, 19 May 1844.

G 64   Marianne Dwight to Frank Dwight, Brook Farm, 29 May 1844.

   Letters from Brook Farm, pp. 17-18.

G 65   Frances Dwight to Frank Dwight, Brook Farm, 2 June 1844.

G 66   Marianne Dwight to Anna Q.T. Parsons, Brook Farm, 4 June 1844.

   Letters from Brook Farm, pp. 18-21.

G 67   Marianne Dwight to Frank Dwight, [Brook Farm], 12 June [1844].

G 68   Marianne Dwight to Frank Dwight, [Brook Farm], 28 June 1844.

G 69   Marianne Dwight to Frank Dwight, Brook Farm, 6 July 1844.

   Letters from Brook Farm, pp. 21-22.

G 70   Marianne Dwight to Anna Q.T. Parsons, Brook Farm, 7 July 1844.

   Letters from Brook Farm, pp. 22-25.

G 71   Marianne Dwight to Frank Dwight, Brook Farm, 7 July 1844.

   Letters from Brook Farm, pp. 25-26.

G 72   Marianne Dwight to Frank Dwight, [Brook Farm], 16 July 1844.

   Letters from Brook Farm, pp. 27-28.

G 73   Marianne Dwight to Frank Dwight, [Brook Farm], [27] August [1844].

   Letters from Brook Farm, p. 29.

G 74   Marianne Dwight to Frank Dwight, [Brook Farm], [31 August 1844].

G 75   Marianne Dwight to Anna Q.T. Parsons, Brook Farm, 3-[5] September 1844.

   Letters from Brook Farm, pp. 34-37.

G 76   Marianne Dwight to Frank Dwight, [Brook Farm], [5 September 1844].

   Letters from Brook Farm, pp. 37-38.

G 77   Marianne Dwight to Anna Q.T. Parsons, Brook Farm, 18 September [1844].

   Letters from Brook Farm, pp. 38-40.

G 78   Marianne Dwight to Frank Dwight, [Brook Farm], 18-[19] September [1844].

   Dated "19 September 1844" in Letters from Brook Farm, pp. 40-42.

G 79   Marianne Dwight to Frank Dwight, [Brook Farm], [9 October 1844].

   Letters from Brook Farm, p. 42.

G 80   Anna Q.T. Parsons to Marianne Dwight, n.p., 16 October 1844.

G 81   Marianne Dwight to Frank Dwight, [Brook Farm], 16 October 1844.

G 82   Marianne Dwight to Anna Q.T. Parsons, Brook Farm, 29 October [1844].

   Letters from Brook Farm, pp. 44-47.

G 83   Marianne Dwight to Frank Dwight, Brook Farm, 1 November 1844.

   Letters from Brook Farm, pp. 47-48.

G 84   Marianne Dwight to Frank Dwight, [Brook Farm], 14 November [1844].

   Letters from Brook Farm, pp. 48-49.

G 85   Anna Q.T. Parsons to Marianne Dwight, Hingham, Massachusetts, 18 November 1844.

G 86   Anna Q.T. Parsons to Marianne Dwight, n.p., [December 1844?].

G 87   Anna Q.T. Parsons to Marianne Dwight, Haverhill, Massachusetts, [December 1844?].

G 88   Anna Q.T. Parsons to Marianne Dwight, n.p., [December 1844?].

G 89   Marianne Dwight to Frank Dwight, [Brook Farm], [4 December 1844].

   Letters from Brook Farm, pp. 49-50.

G 90   Marianne Dwight to Anna Q.T. Parsons, Brook Farm, 14 December 1844.

   Letters from Brook Farm, pp. 50-52.

G 91   Marianne Dwight to Frank Dwight, [Brook Farm], [16 December 1844?].

G 92   Marianne Dwight to Anna Q.T. Parsons, Brook Farm, 22 December 1844.

   Letters from Brook Farm, pp. 53-55.

G 93   Marianne Dwight to Anna Q.T. Parsons, Brook Farm, 30 December 1844.

   Letters from Brook Farm, pp. 55-58.

G 94   Marianne Dwight to Anna Q.T. Parsons, [Brook Farm], [January 1845?].

G 95   Marianne Dwight to Frank Dwight, [Brook Farm], [5 January 1845].

   Letters from Brook Farm, pp. 58-59.

G 96   Marianne Dwight to Anna Q.T. Parsons, [Brook Farm], 6 January 1845.

   Letters from Brook Farm, pp. 59-61.

G 97   Marianne Dwight to Frank Dwight, Brook Farm, 8 January 1845.

   Letters from Brook Farm, p. 61.

G 98   Marianne Dwight to Frank Dwight, [Brook Farm], 11 January [1845].

G 99   Marianne Dwight to Anna Q.T. Parsons, [Brook Farm], 14 January [1845].

G 100   Marianne Dwight to Frank Dwight, [Brook Farm], 15 January [1845].

   Letters from Brook Farm, p. 64.

G 101   Anna Q.T. Parsons to Marianne Dwight, Boston, 18 January 1845.

G 102   Marianne Dwight to Frank Dwight, [Brook Farm], 27 February [1845].

G 103   Marianne Dwight to Anna Q.T. Parsons, [Brook Farm], 9 March [1845].

   Letters from Brook Farm, pp. 85-87.

G 104   Marianne Dwight to Frank Dwight, Brook Farm, 21 February [1845].

G 105   Marianne Dwight to Frank Dwight, [Brook Farm], [20 February 1845?].

G 106   Marianne Dwight to Anna Q.T. Parsons, Brook Farm, [27?] February [1845].

   Letters from Brook Farm, pp. 80-82.

G 107   Marianne Dwight to Frank Dwight, Brook Farm, 15-[16] February 1845.

   Letters from Brook Farm, pp. 77-80.

G 108   Marianne Dwight to Frank Dwight, Brook Farm, [6 February 1845].

Letters from Brook Farm, pp. 76-77.

G 109   Marianne Dwight to Frank Dwight, Brook Farm, 30 March [1845].

Letters from Brook Farm, pp. 87-88.

G 110   Marianne Dwight to Frank Dwight, [Brook Farm], [April 1845?].

G 111   Marianne Dwight to Frank Dwight, Brook Farm, 13 March 1845.

G 112   Anna Q.T. Parsons to Marianne Dwight, n.p., [11 March 1845].

G 113   Marianne Dwight to Anna Q.T. Parsons, Brook Farm, 19 January 1845.

Letters from Brook Farm, pp. 64-67.

G 114   Marianne Dwight to Anna Q.T. Parsons, [Brook Farm], 24 January [1845].

Letters from Brook Farm, pp. 68-70.

G 115   Marianne Dwight to Frank Dwight, Brook Farm, 26 January [1845].

Letters from Brook Farm, pp. 70-72.

G 116   Marianne Dwight to Frank Dwight, Brook Farm, 27 January 1845.

Letters from Brook Farm, pp. 72-76.

G 117   Marianne Dwight to Frank Dwight, Brook Farm, 25 March [1845].

G 118   Marianne Dwight to Frank Dwight, [Brook Farm], [19 March 1845].

Letters from Brook Farm, p. 87.

G 119   Anna Q.T. Parsons to Marianne Dwight, n.p., [April 1845?].

G 120   Anna Q.T. Parsons to Marianne Dwight, n.p., [April 1845?].

G 121   Anna Q.T. Parsons to Marianne Dwight, n.p., [January 1846?].

G 122   Marianne Dwight to Anna Q.T. Parsons, Brook Farm, 8-[10] April [1845].

Letters from Brook Farm, pp. 88-93.

G 123   Anna Q.T. Parsons to Marianne Dwight, Boston, 21 April 1845.

G 124   Anna Q.T. Parsons to Frank Dwight, [Brook Farm], [May 1845?].

G 125   Marianne Dwight to Frank Dwight, [Brook Farm], 30 April 1845.

       Letters from Brook Farm, pp. 93-94.

G 126   Marianne Dwight to Frank Dwight, [Brook Farm], 29 April [1845].

G 127   Marianne Dwight to Frank Dwight, [Brook Farm], 22 April [1845].

G 128   Marianne Dwight to Anna Q.T. Parsons, [Brook Farm], 14 May [1845].

       Letters from Brook Farm, pp. 96-97.

G 129   Marianne Dwight to Frank Dwight, [Brook Farm], 14 May [1845].

G 130   Marianne Dwight to Frank Dwight, [Brook Farm], 15 May [1845].

G 131   Marianne Dwight to Anna Q.T. Parsons, Brook Farm, 16 May [1845].

       Letters from Brook Farm, pp. 97-100.

G 132   Marianne Dwight to Frank Dwight, Brook Farm, 18 May [1845].

G 133   Anna Q.T. Parsons to Marianne Dwight, n.p., 18 May 1845.

G 134   Marianne Dwight to Frank Dwight, [Brook Farm], [2 July 1845].

       Dated "July [1845]" in Letters from Brook Farm, p. 106.

G 135   Marianne Dwight to Anna Q.T. Parsons, [Brook Farm], 25 May [1845].

       Letters from Brook Farm, pp. 100-102.

G 136   Anna Q.T. Parsons to Marianne Dwight, n.p., [July 1845].

G 137   Marianne Dwight to Frank Dwight, [Brook Farm], 6 June [1845].

       Letters from Brook Farm, pp. 102-103.

G 138   Marianne Dwight to Frank Dwight, Brook Farm, 9 July 1845.

G 139   Marianne Dwight to Frank Dwight, [Brook Farm], [1 July 1845].

G 140   Anna Q.T. Parsons to Marianne Dwight, n.p., [June 1845].

G 141   Marianne Dwight to Anna Q.T. Parsons, Brook Farm, 1 August 1845.

       Letters from Brook Farm, pp. 106-108.

G 142   Marianne Dwight to Anna Q.T. Parsons, [Brook Farm], [December 1846?].

G 143   Marianne Dwight to Anna Q.T. Parsons, Brook Farm, [December 1846?].

G 144   Marianne Dwight to Anna Q.T. Parsons, [Brook Farm], [March 1846?].

G 145   Marianne Dwight to Frank Dwight, [Brook Farm], 6 August 1845.

   Letters from Brook Farm, pp. 108–110.

G 146   Marianne Dwight to Anna Q.T. Parsons, Brook Farm, 11 August [1845].

   Letters from Brook Farm, pp. 110–114.

G 147   Marianne Dwight to Anna Q.T. Parsons, [Brook Farm], 5 October 1845.

   Letters from Brook Farm, pp. 119–122.

G 148   Anna Q.T. Parsons to Marianne Dwight, Hingham, 26 August 1845.

G 149   Marianne Dwight to Anna Q.T. Parsons, Brook Farm, 28 September [1845].

   Letters from Brook Farm, pp. 118–119.

G 150   Marianne Dwight to Anna Q.T. Parsons, [Brook Farm], [September 1845?].

   Letters from Brook Farm, p. 117.

G 151   Marianne Dwight to Anna Q.T. Parsons, Brook Farm, [31 August 1845].

   Letters from Brook Farm, pp. 114–116.

G 152   Marianne Dwight to Anna Q.T. Parsons, Brook Farm, 30 August [1845?].

G 153   Anna Q.T. Parsons to Marianne Dwight, Boston, 18 October 1845.

G 154   Marianne Dwight to Anna Q.T. Parsons, Brook Farm, 19 October 1845.

   Letters from Brook Farm, pp. 122–126.

G 155   Marianne Dwight to Frank Dwight, [Brook Farm], 10 November [1845].

Letters from Brook Farm, pp. 128–130.

G 156 Marianne Dwight to Frank Dwight, [Brook Farm], [11–12 November 1845].

Letters from Brook Farm, pp. 130–132.

G 157 Marianne Dwight to Frank Dwight, [Brook Farm], 18 November [1845].

G 158 Marianne Dwight to Anna Q.T. Parsons, [Brook Farm], 9 November 1845.

Letters from Brook Farm, pp. 126–128.

G 159 Marianne Dwight to Frank Dwight, [Brook Farm], [November 1845].

G 160 Marianne Dwight to Anna Q.T. Parsons, [Brook Farm], 23 November 1845.

Letters from Brook Farm, pp. 132–135.

G 161 Marianne Dwight to Frank Dwight, [Brook Farm], [November 1845?].

G 162 Marianne Dwight to Frank Dwight, Brook Farm, [3 November 1845?].

G 163 Marianne Dwight to Frank Dwight, Brook Farm, 31 December 1845.

Letters from Brook Farm, pp. 142–143.

G 164 Marianne Dwight to Frank Dwight, Brook Farm, 14 January [1846?].

G 165 Anna Q.T. Parsons to Marianne Dwight, n.p., [January 1848?].

G 166 Marianne Dwight to Frank Dwight, Brook Farm, 17 March 1846.

Letters from Brook Farm, pp. 152–155.

G 167 Marianne Dwight to Anna Q.T. Parsons, [Brook Farm], 17 March [1846].

Letters from Brook Farm, pp. 151–152.

G 168 Marianne Dwight to Frank Dwight, [Brook Farm], 12 March [1846].

Letters from Brook Farm, pp. 149–150.

G 169 Marianne Dwight to Anna Q.T. Parsons, [Brook Farm], [March 1846].

   Letters from Brook Farm, p. 150.

G 170 Marianne Dwight to Anna Q.T. Parsons, Brook Farm, 4 March 1846.

   Letters from Brook Farm, pp. 145-149.

G 171 Marianne Dwight to Anna Q.T. Parsons, Brook Farm, 1 March 1846.

   Letters from Brook Farm, pp. 143-145.

G 172 Marianne Dwight to Anna Q.T. Parsons, Brook Farm, 19 April 1846.

   Letters from Brook Farm, pp. 163-166.

G 173 Marianne Dwight to Anna Q.T. Parsons, Brook Farm, 24 April 1846.

   Letters from Brook Farm, pp. 166-169.

G 174 Anna Q.T. Parsons to Lucy Goddard, Brook Farm, 4 August 1846.

G 175 Marianne Dwight to Anna Q.T. Parsons, [Brook Farm], [December 1846?].

G 176 Marianne Dwight to Anna Q.T. Parsons, [Brook Farm], [December 1846?].

G 177 Marianne Dwight to Frank Dwight, [Brook Farm], [17 October 1846].

   Letters from Brook Farm, pp. 173-174.

G 178 Marianne Dwight to Frank Dwight, [Brook Farm], 7 April [1846].

   Letters from Brook Farm, pp. 162-163.

G 179 Marianne Dwight to Anna Q.T. Parsons, Brook Farm, 27 March [1846].

G 180 Marianne Dwight to Frank Dwight, [Brook Farm], [4 March 1845?].

G 181 Marianne Dwight to Frank Dwight, [Brook Farm], [17 March 1845?].

G 182 Marianne Dwight Orvis to Anna Q.T. Parsons, [Brook Farm], [January 1847?].

Marianne Dwight had married John Orvis at Brook Farm on 24 December 1846.

G 183   Marianne Dwight Orvis to Anna Q.T. Parsons, [Brook Farm], [January 1847?].

G 184   Marianne Dwight Orvis to Anna Q.T. Parsons, [Brook Farm], 4 February [1847?].

G 185   Marianne Dwight Orvis to Anna Q.T. Parsons, Brook Farm, 16 May [1847].

G 186   Marianne Dwight Orvis to Anna Q.T. Parsons, Brook Farm, 1 July 1847.

G 187   Anna Q.T. Parsons to Marianne Dwight Orvis, n.p., [1847?].

G 188   Marianne Dwight Orvis to Anna Q.T. Parsons, Brook Farm, [July 1847].

G 189   Marianne Dwight Orvis to Anna Q.T. Parsons, Brook Farm, 18 July 1847.

G 190   Marianne Dwight Orvis to Anna Q.T. Parsons, Brook Farm, 17 May 1847.

G 191   Marianne Dwight to Anna Q.T. Parsons, [Brook Farm], 4 December [1846?].

G 192   Marianne Dwight Orvis to Anna Q.T. Parsons, [Brook Farm], 26 December 1846.

G 193   Marianne Dwight to Anna Q.T. Parsons, [Brook Farm], [Spring 1846].

Letters from Brook Farm, pp. 155–158.

G 194   Marianne Dwight to Frank Dwight, [Brook Farm], [August 1845?].

G 195   Marianne Dwight to Anna Q.T. Parsons, Brook Farm, 7 December 1845.

Letters from Brook Farm, pp. 136–139.

G 196   Marianne Dwight to Anna Q.T. Parsons, [Brook Farm], 12 December 1845.

Letters from Brook Farm, pp. 139–142.

G 197   Marianne Dwight to Anna Q.T. Parsons, Brook Farm, 22 March 1846.

Letters from Brook Farm, pp. 159–162.

G 198 Anna Q.T. Parsons to Marianne Dwight, n.p., 8 March 1846.

G 199 Anna Q.T. Parsons to Marianne Dwight, Boston, 10 March 1846.

G 200 Anna Q.T. Parsons to Marianne Dwight, n.p., 22 December 1844.

G 201 Day Book. Group of Dinner Waiters. May 1845–April 1846.

Records of those Brook Farmers who served as dinner waiters (20 pp.).

G 202 Day Book. Printing Group. April 1846–October 1846.

Record of those Brook Farmers who helped in the printing plant (11 pp.).

REEL TWO

G 203 Day Book B. Brook Farm. 5 January 1845–June 1847.

Ledger-type book recording the daily purchases and sales for the community (135 pp.). Also includes a list of members. At the end is a non-related item, the account book of Joshua Buttrick of Concord, Massachusetts, from 1851 to 1861 (22 pp.).

G 204 Journal B. Brook Farm. November 1844–October 1846.

Ledger-type book recording the daily statements of profit and loss for the community (250 pp.). Also includes a list of members.

G 205 Constitution and Minutes of the Brook Farm Association. January 1843–August 1847.

Traces, through minutes of the meetings, the progress of Brook Farm from an agricultural and industrial association to a phalanx, including copies of the constitutions (220 pp.).

G 206 Miscellaneous manuscripts, undated.

Two items: "Records lent by Miss Ellis" about Brook Farm, mainly secondary information (2 pp.); a legal opinion about the state of Brook Farm's stocks (8 pp.).

MIDDLEBURY COLLEGE LIBRARY

The Middlebury College Library contains a number of letters dealing with Brook Farm in its Abernethy Library of American Literature. Photocopies of the manuscript letters can be ordered at a nominal cost.

G 207   John Allen to Mehitable Eastman, Menonia, Massachusetts, 1 October 1845. M-2.220.1.

  Allen, an abolitionist minister, came to Brook Farm in March 1845, after his wife died. This letter gives Allen's comments about the goals of Brook Farm.

G 208   John Allen to Mehitable Eastman, Brook Farm, 2 November-1 December 1845. M-2.220.3.

  Allen describes the smallpox epidemic at Brook Farm.

G 209   John Allen to John Sullivan Dwight, South Danvers, Massachusetts, 28 December 1845. M-2.220.5.

  Allen wishes the Brook Farmers a happy New Year, and sends on the names of new subscribers to the Harbinger.

G 210   John Allen to Marianne Dwight, Saxton's River, Vermont, [15? February 1846?]. M-2.220.6.

  A newsletter describing Allen's lecture tour on behalf of associationism.

G 211   John Allen to Marianne Dwight, North Bennington, Vermont, 9 March 1846. M-2.220.7.

  Allen describes his shock upon receiving her letter about the Phalanstery fire, and offers his sympathy.

G 212   William Henry Channing to John Sullivan Dwight, Brattleboro, Vermont, 18 January 1846. M-2.223.

  Channing's ill-health prevents him from lecturing more on behalf of Brook Farm than he has already done.

G 213   Sophia Eastman to Mehitable Eastman, West Roxbury, 25 July 1843. M-2.225.

  Eastman gives details about daily life at Brook Farm. Quoted in Sams, Autobiography of Brook Farm (D 74), pp. 80-82, and Webber, Escape to Utopia (D 89), pp. 180-182.

G 214 Convers Francis to Theodore Parker, Cambridge, 22–29 June 1844. M–2.226.

Francis describes a visit to Brook Farm when he preached there. He feels a "distrust" of Fourier.

G 215 James Kay to John Sullivan Dwight, Philadelphia, 14 March 1845. M–2.229.1.

Printed in full in Gohdes, "Three Letters by James Kay Dealing with Brook Farm" (B 57), 379–380.

G 216 James Kay to John Sullivan Dwight, Philadelphia, 10 May 1846. M–2.229.2.

Printed in full in Gohdes, "Three Letters by James Kay Dealing with Brook Farm" (B 57), 381–384.

G 217 James Kay to Marianne Dwight, Philadelphia, 27 September 1846. M–2.229.3.

Printed in full in Gohdes, "Three Letters by James Kay Dealing with Brook Farm" (B 57), 386–388.

G 218 John Orvis to John Sullivan Dwight, Newburyport, Massachusetts, 16 January 1847. M–2.230.1.

Orvis was in his late twenties when he arrived at Brook Farm in late 1843. Already committed to the anti-slavery cause, he soon found himself lecturing on Fourierism and Brook Farm across New England. This letter describes one of his lecture tours and his canvassing for subscribers to the Harbinger.

G 219 John Orvis to Marianne Dwight Orvis, Edgartown, Massachusetts, 8 March 1847. M–2.230.4.

Orvis had married Marianne Dwight on 24 December 1846. This letter describes his lecture tour. Quoted in Sams, Autobiography of Brook Farm (D 74), pp. 202–203.

G 220 John Orvis to Marianne Dwight Orvis, Rochester, New York, 31 August–1 September 1847. M–2.230.7.

Orvis describes his lecture tour. Quoted in Sams, Autobiography of Brook Farm (D 74), pp. 205–206.

G 221 John Orvis to Marianne Dwight Orvis, Waterloo, New York, 5 September 1847. M–2.230.8.

Orvis describes his lecture tour.

G 222   John Orvis to Marianne Dwight Orvis, Manchester, New York,
        9 December 1847. M-2.230.10.

        Orvis describes his lecture tour.

G 223   Marianne Dwight to John Allen, [Brook Farm], 3 March [1846].
        M-2.231.

        The sister of John Sullivan Dwight, Marianne arrived
        at Brook Farm in the fall of 1843. This letter describes
        the fire at the Phalanstery.

G 224   Anna Q.T. Parsons to Marianne Dwight, n.p., 4 March 1846.
        M-2.233.

        Parsons was engaged in many reform activities. This
        letter asks about the Phalanstery fire and the future
        of Brook Farm.

G 225   George Ripley to Phineas Eastman, [Brook Farm], 24 November
        1843. M-2.234.1.

        Eastman's daughter is unable to profit from schooling
        at Brook Farm and Ripley requests that she be withdrawn.
        Quoted in Sams, Autobiography of Brook Farm (D 74), pp.
        85-86.

UNIVERSITY OF NOTRE DAME LIBRARY

The Microfilm Edition of the Orestes Augustus Brownson Papers, those manuscripts and copies of manuscripts deposited at the University of Notre Dame Library, is available for purchase or through interlibrary loan on positive microfilm. The contents of each reel are listed at the beginning, and the first reel contains a list of all material in the edition. A printed guide to the collection is available; see B 9. Much of this material was used in Henry F. Brownson, Orestes A. Brownson's Early Life (B 8).

G 226   George Ripley to Brownson, Brook Farm, 18 December 1842.
        Reel One, "Correspondence, 1823-1842."

        Printed in full in Orestes A. Brownson's Early Life,
        pp. 311-315.

G 227   Hugh A. Garland to Brownson, Petersburg, Virginia, 28
        November 1842. Reel One, "Correspondence, 1823-1842."

Printed in full in <u>Orestes A. Brownson's Early Life</u>, pp. 308-311.

G 228 John Hecker to Brownson, New York, 7 January 1843. Reel Two, "Correspondence, 1843-1849."

Printed in full in <u>Orestes A. Brownson's Early Life</u>, pp. 501-503.

G 229 George Ripley to Brownson, Brook Farm, 22 July 1843. Reel Two, "Correspondence, 1843-1849."

Printed in full in <u>Orestes A. Brownson's Early Life</u>, pp. 315-316.

G 230 Albert Brisbane to Brownson, [New York], [1844]. Reel Two, "Correspondence, 1843-1849."

Brisbane comments on the progress of associationism.

G 231 Albert Brisbane to Brownson, New York, 21 February 1844. Reel Two, "Correspondence, 1843-1849."

Brisbane comments on the progress of associationism.

INDEX

INDEX

Abel, Darrel, A 55.

Abernethy Library of American Literature. See Middlebury College Library.

Academy, D 82.

Adams, Raymond, D 4.

Agricultural Seminary, D 91.

ALA Booklist, A 133, D 15.

Alberti, Charles Edward, D 5.

Albree, John, A 39.

Alcott, Amos Bronson, D 82; Compared with Emerson, D 29; Compared with Ripley, D 29; Description of, A 93, B 58, G 39; Journals by, D 74; Letters by, B 3.

Alcott, Mrs. Amos Bronson [Abigail]: Description of Brook Farm, B 2.

Allen, John, A 102; Letters by, G 30, G 207-G 211; Letters to, G 223.

Allen, William: Letters by, D 26.

Amana Colony, D 95.

American Heritage, D 25.

American Literature, A 47, A 77, A 120, E 8.

American Lyceum, D 91.

American Mercury, F 5.

American Transcendental Quarterly, A 105, D 63.

American Union of Associationists, E 1.

Anderson, Judith Müller, A 56.

Annals of the American Academy, A 22.

Arena, A 22.

Arnold, William Harris, D 6.

Associationism, A 14, A 22, A 45, A 102, C 5, C 8, C 22, D 21, D 74, G 21, G 23, G 29, G 30, G 210; Brisbane on, A 22, G 15-G 17, G 230, G 231; W.H. Channing on, A 22, B 18; Dana on, A 35, A 36, G 47; J.S. Dwight on, A 22, A 41, A 42; Greeley on, A 22; Harbinger and, E 1, E 4, E 14; Whittier on, C 27.

Atlantic Monthly, A 43, A 127, A 128, A 134, A 135, B 23.

Ave Maria, A 125.

Barrows, Belle C., A 8.

Bates, Ernest Sutherland, D 7.

Beatty, Lillian, A 57.

Bell, George H., A 58.

Bellamy, Edward, B 64.

Bemis, Edward W., A 24.

Bestor, Arthur E., Jr., D 8, D 9.

Betham-Edwards, M., A 9.

Blackwell, Anna: Recollections of Brook Farm, A 9.

Blair, Nore Schelter: Recollections of Brook Farm, A 97.

Blaxton, C., C 9.

Bode, Carl, D 74.

Böhmer, Lina, A 59.
Bonham, Martha E., D 10.
Book Buyer, D 82.
Book-Lover, C 16.
Bookman, D 17.
Books [New York Herald Tribune], D 15.
Boston Evening Transcript, A 4, A 22, A 25, A 99, A 129–A 132, C 9, D 3, D 15, D 82, F 6.
Boston Herald, A 20, A 22, D 40, D 82.
Boston Public Library, D 42, D 43, G 1–G 32.
Boston Public Library Quarterly, D 21.
Boston Sunday Globe, D 38.
Boughton, Willis, D 11.
Bounds, Harrison, A 60.
Bowdoin Prize Essays, A 111.
Boynton, Percy H., B 27.
Bradford, George P.: Recollections of Brook Farm, A 10, A 11.
Bradley, Lawrence J., B 9.
Bridge, Horatio, A 61.
Brisbane, Albert, B 4, B 5, B 9, D 26, D 82; Description of, A 48; Letters by, G 15–G 17, G 230, G 231; On associationism, A 22, E 1, G 15–G 17, G 230, G 231; On Fourierism, C 15.
Brisbane, Redelia, B 4.
Broadway Journal, C 24.
Brook Farm Association for Industry and Education, D 74; Constitution of, A 12, A 13, B 18, C 3, C 4, C 7, D 47, D 74, G 205.

Brook Farm, Buildings and Land, D 3, D 30, D 31, D 38, D 44, D 45, D 56, D 57, D 71, D 72, D 82, D 83, D 94, F 3, G 2. See also Phalanstery.
Brook Farm Centennial Committee, D 12.
Brook Farm, Fire at, A 6, A 22, A 104, A 131–A 133, C 2, D 52, D 74, D 95, G 24, G 211, G 223, G 224.
Brook Farm Phalanx, A 22, B 15, D 46, D 74, E 1; Constitution of, A 3, A 14, C 6, G 205.
Brook Farm School, A 103, B 8, B 57, C 1, C 2, C 10, D 82, G 6, G 12, G 32, G 33; Advertisement for, A 2; Kindergarten, A 4; Recollections of, A 49, A 97, A 129, A 130, A 134, A 135. See also Education at Brook Farm.
Brook Farm: The Amusing and Memorable of American Country Life, F 1.
Brooks, Tom, D 64.
Brooks, Van Wyck, A 48, D 13, D 14.
Brown, Arthur W., B 38.
Brown, John Stillman, A 15, G 34; Letters by, G 36, G 38, G 43, G 45; Letters to, G 33, G 35, G 39, G 41, G 42, G 44.
Brown, Mary R.: Letters by, G 35, G 42, G 44; Letters to, G 36, G 38, G 39, G 43, G 45.
Browning, Robert, D 39.
Brownson, Henry F., B 8, B 9, G 226–G 229.
Brownson, Orestes A., B 6–B 13; Description of, A 94; Letters to, B 6, B 8, B 9, G 226–G 231; Ripley and, B 8.
Brownson's Quarterly Review, B 7.
Bruce, Georgiana. See Georgiana Bruce Kirby.

Bulletin of the Salem Public Library, D 1.

Burton, Katherine, A 87, A 122, A 123; Paradise Planters: The Story of Brook Farm, D 15.

Butterfield, Rebecca Codman: Recollections of Brook Farm, A 16, A 17.

Buttrick, Joshua, G 203.

Byam, Milton S., D 64.

C. See John A. Collins.

Cabot, James Elliot, B 28.

Calverton, V.F., D 16.

Cameron, Kenneth Walter, A 105, A 114, B 29, D 63; Transcendental Log, A 1, A 64, A 105, B 26, D 2, D 31.

Cannon, Lee E., D 64.

Cantwell, Robert, A 62.

Carew, Harold D., D 17.

Carlson, Oliver, B 5.

Carlyle, Thomas: Letters by, C 16; Letters to, B 22; On Ripley, C 12.

Carter, Robert: Recollections of Brook Farm, B 16.

Cary, Edward, A 30.

Catholic Digest, D 67.

Catholic World, A 124, D 15, D 56, D 60, D 64.

Catholicism, A 123–A 125, B 12, D 65, D 67. See also Orestes A. Brownson, Isaac T. Hecker, Sophia Willard Dana Ripley.

Century Magazine, A 10, A 71, B 16.

Chadwick, John White, A 22, D 82.

Channing, Reverend William Ellery, C 21.

Channing, William Henry, B 17, B 19, D 32; Curtis on, A 25; Description of, A 48; Letters by, B 19, G 18, G 28, G 212; On associationism, A 22, B 18; On Fuller, B 40; Socialism and, D 66.

Child, Lydia Maria: Letters by, G 10.

Christian Century, D 15, D 26, D 64.

Christian Examiner, A 101.

Christian Leader, D 95.

Christian Register, A 8, A 22.

Christian Science Monitor, D 15, D 26.

Chubb, Edwin Watts, A 18.

Clark, Jerome L., D 18.

Clarke, Helen Archibald, A 63.

Clarke, James Freeman: On Fuller, B 40.

Clarke, Mrs. James Freeman, C 25.

Clarke, Sarah: Letters by, C 20; On Ripley, C 20.

Codman, John Thomas: Brook Farm, A 19, A 22, D 74; Letters by, A 24; Letters to, A 19; Recollections of Brook Farm, A 4, A 20, A 21, A 23.

Coleman, Caryl, A 124.

Collins, John A.: Description of Brook Farm, B 14, B 15.

Colt, Caroline Henshaw, G 10.

Coming Age, A 21, A 23.

Commonweal, D 15.

Communism: Emerson and, B 2.

Communitarianism, D 4, D 23, D 88.

Communitism, D 80.

Communitist, B 14, B 15.

Conservator, A 22, A 40, D 82.

"Constitution and Minutes of the Brook Farm Association," G 205.

Conway, Moncure Daniel, A 64, A 65, B 30.

Cooke, George Willis, A 4, A 31, D 19, E 3; Early Letters of George Wm. Curtis to John S. Dwight, A 25, A 31, D 74; John Sullivan Dwight, A 44, B 29, D 74.

Coverdale, Miles, A 82. See also Nathaniel Hawthorne, The Blithedale Romance.

Cranch, Christopher Pearse, B 21; Curtis on, A 25, B 20; Description of, A 95; Letters by, B 21.

Crawford, Mary Caroline, A 16, D 20.

Cromphout, Gustaaf Van, A 66.

Crowe, Charles R., A 107, A 108, D 21-D 24.

Current Literature, D 81.

Curtis, Alice Cabell, A 67.

Curtis, Burrill, A 30.

Curtis, Edith Roelker, D 25; A Season in Utopia: The Story of Brook Farm, A 68, D 26.

Curtis, George William, A 18, A 30, A 32, A 34, D 52; Compared with Parker, A 33; Compared with Ripley, A 33; Description of, A 134-A 136; Early Letters of George Wm. Curtis to John S. Dwight, A 25, A 31, D 74; "Editor's Easy Chair," A 26-A 29, A 109, B 20, B 39; Letters by, A 31, A 88, G 11, G 40: see also Early Letters of George Wm. Curtis to John S. Dwight; On W.H. Channing, A 25; On Cranch, A 25, B 20; On Dana, A 25; On Emerson, A 25; On Fuller, B 39; On Hawthorne, A 25, A 26; On Hecker, A 25, A 88; Recollections of Brook Farm, A 26-A 29, A 32, A 88; Transcendentalism and, A 33.

Cushman, Herbert Ernest, F 2.

Cutter, M. Gertrude, A 17.

D., R.T., D 15.

Daily life at Brook Farm, A 9, A 10, A 17, A 21, A 22, A 25, A 40, A 48, A 50-A 52, A 54, A 92-A 97, A 127-A 136, D 74, D 82, D 89, G 7, G 36-G 38, G 42, G 52-G 206, G 213.

Dall, Caroline, C 13.

Dana, Charles A., A 38, B 53, D 52, D 74, G 35; Curtis on, A 25; Description of, A 40, A 48, A 93, A 131, A 132, A 134-A 136; Dwight on, A 1; Emerson on, A 1; Greeley and, B 48; Greeley on, B 53; Harbinger and, E 11; Hawthorne and, A 77; Lectures by, A 35, A 36, A 38; Letters by, A 37-A 39, G 20, G 33, G 37, G 46-G 51; Marriage of, G 24; On associationism, A 35, A 36, G 47; On Fourier, A 5; On Fourierism, A 37; Recollections of Brook Farm, A 38.

Dana, Gorham, D 27.

Dana family: On S. Ripley, A 125, A 126.

"Day Book. Group of Dinner Waiters," G 201.

"Day Book. Printing Group," G 202.

"Day Book B. Brook Farm," G 203.

Delano, Sterling F., E 4.

Demorest's Monthly Magazine, B 51.

Dial [Boston], B 59-B 62; Harbinger and, E 3; Ripley on, G 1, G 3.

Dial [Chicago], A 22.

Diaz, Abby Morton: Recollections of Brook Farm, A 4.

Diebitsch, Roberta Watterson, D 28.

Dinner Waiters Group, G 201.

Doon, John Anthony, Jr., D 29.

Dorchester News, D 31.

Doucet, J. Homer, A 22; Recollections of Brook Farm, A 40.

Drake, Francis S., D 30

Drama at Brook Farm, D 33.

Driscoll, Annette S., A 125.

Duffy, John J., A 110, C 18.

Dwight, Frances: Letters by, G 65.

Dwight, Frank: Letters to, A 48, G 58, G 61, G 64, G 65, G 67–G 69, G 71–G 74, G 76, G 78, G 79, G 81, G 83, G 84, G 89, G 91, G 95, G 97, G 98, G 100, G 102, G 104, G 105, G 107–G 111, G 115–G 118, G 124–G 127, G 129, G 130, G 132, G 134, G 137–G 139, G 145, G 155–G 157, G 159, G 161–G 164, G 166, G 168, G 177, G 178, G 180, G 181, G 194.

Dwight, John Sullivan, A 43–A 45, A 48, D 42, D 74, G 223; Description of, A 48, A 94, A 136; German literature and, A 47; Harbinger and, E 11; Lectures by, A 42; Letters by, A 44–A 46, G 9, G 13, G 23; Letters to, A 25, A 31, A 100, B 19, B 21, B 29, B 57, D 42, D 43, G 1–G 8, G 10–G 22, G 24–G 32, G 209, G 212, G 215, G 216, G 218; On associationism, A 22, A 41, A 42; On Dana, A 1; Recollections of Brook Farm, A 1, A 8.

Dwight, Marianne, G 182; Letters by, G 52–G 62, G 64, G 66–G 79, G 81–G 84, G 89–G 100, G 102–G 111, G 113–G 118, G 122, G 125–G 132, G 134, G 135, G 137–G 139, G 141–G 147, G 149–G 152, G 154–G 164, G 166–G 173, G 175–G 186, G 188–G 197, G 223: see also Letters from Brook Farm; Letters from Brook Farm, A 22, A 48, D 26, D 74, G 55, G 56, G 58–G 60, G 62, G 64, G 66, G 69–G 73, G 75–G 79, G 82–G 84, G 89, G 90, G 92, G 93, G 95–G 97, G 100, G 103, G 106–G 109, G 113–G 116, G 118, G 122, G 125, G 128, G 131, G 134, G 135, G 137, G 141, G 145–G 147, G 149–G 151, G 154–G 156, G 158, G 160, G 163, G 166–G 173, G 177, G 178, G 193, G 195–G 197; Letters to, B 57, G 63, G 80, G 85–G 88, G 101, G 112, G 119–G 121, G 123, G 133, G 136, G 140, G 148, G 153, G 165, G 187, G 198–G 200, G 210, G 211, G 217, G 219–G 222, G 224.

Eastman, Mehitable: Letters to, G 207, G 208, G 213.

Eastman, Phineas: Letters to, G 225.

Eastman, Sophia: Letters by, D 89, G 213.

Eaton, Walter Prichard, D 15.

Education at Brook Farm, A 42. A 117, B 6, C 11, D 5, D 74, D 91, D 92, G 225. See also Brook Farm School.

Edwards, Channing, A 111.

Elliott, Walter, A 88, D 76.

Ellis, Miss, G 206.

Emerson, Ralph Waldo, A 34, B 23, B 27, B 31, B 33–B 35, C 16, D 74; Communism and, B 32; Compared with Alcott, D 29; Compared with Hawthorne, A 66, A 76; Compared with Ripley, D 29; Curtis on, A 25; Description of, G 44; Journals by, B 24, B 28, D 74; Lectures by, B 26; Letters by, B 22, B 25, B 28, B 29, D 47, D 74; Letters to, D 47; On Dana, A 1; On Fuller, B 40; On

Harbinger, B 29; On Ripley, B 22; Recollections of Brook Farm, A 1.

Emerson Society Quarterly, A 46, A 69, A 110, B 29, B 34.

ESQ: A Journal of the American Renaissance, D 80.

Evening Post [New York], A 105, D 83.

Every Saturday Journal, A 64.

F., D 31.

Fertig, Walter L., A 45.

Finch, John: Description of Brook Farm, B 36, B 37.

Firkins, O.W., B 31.

Flanagan, John T., B 32.

Flint, Reverend James: Letters to, G 9.

Foote, Mary Wilder: Letters by, C 14.

Foster, Charles H., D 26.

Fourier, Charles, A 5, A 14, A 22, B 49, C 15, D 32, G 214.

Fourierism, A 14, A 22, A 36, A 37, B 4, B 7, B 15, B 57, B 60, C 8, C 15, D 7, D 9, D 16, D 18, D 37, D 46, D 48, D 62, D 64–D 66, D 68, D 70, D 73, D 74, D 82, D 88, G 13, G 218; Brisbane on, C 15; Dana on, A 36, A 37; Greeley and, B 46; Harbinger and, E 4, E 7, E 10, E 15; Hawthorne on, A 74; Ripley and, D 21; G. Sand and, E 10; E. Sue and, E 10, E 15; Transcendentalism and, D 22, D 32.

Francis, Convers: Description of Brook Farm, B 65, G 214; Letters by, G 214; On Fourier, G 214; On Ripley, B 65.

Francis, Richard, D 32.

French-language studies, D 35.

French literature: Harbinger and, E 8–E 10, E 15.

French Review, E 10.

French Revolution: Harbinger on, E 6.

Frothingham, Octavius Brooks, D 47, D 74, E 5; On W.H. Channing, B 19; On Ripley, A 8, A 112, A 113.

Fruitlands Community, B 58, D 80, G 39.

Fuller, Richard F.: Recollections of Brook Farm, B 45.

Fuller, Sarah Margaret, B 38, B 43, B 44, D 74; The Blithedale Romance and, A 81, B 41; W.H. Channing on, B 40; J.F. Clarke on, B 40; Curtis on, B 39; Description of, A 93, A 95, A 127; Description of Brook Farm, B 40; Emerson on, B 40; Greeley and, B 48; Journals by, B 40; Letters by, B 40–B 42, D 43. See also Nathaniel Hawthorne, The Blithedale Romance.

Gafford, Lucile, D 33.

Gallant, Barbara Gans, E 6.

Garland, Hugh A.: Letters by, B 8, G 227.

Garnett, Richard, B 33.

Gaskill, Kate Sloan: Recollections of Brook Farm, A 49.

Geismar, Maxwell, D 15.

Georgia Review, A 66.

German-language studies, A 59, B 43.

German literature: J.S. Dwight and, A 47; Harbinger and, E 18; Ripley and, A 120.

Gidez, Richard B., D 34.

Gilman, William H., B 24.

Girard, William, D 35.

Goddard, Lucy: Letters to, G 174.

Godwin, Parke: Letters by, G 31; On Fourierism, C 15.

Gohdes, Clarence L.F., A 115, B 57, E 7, G 215–G 217.

Going, Maud, D 36.

Goldstein, Jonah, D 37.

Good Health, A 17.

Goodman, Ellen, D 38.

Gordon, George Henry, F 3.

Gordon, Joseph T., A 69.

Grant, Elijah P., D 74.

Greeley, Horace, B 47, D 26, D 52, G 23; Dana and, B 48; Description of, A 127, A 133; Fuller and, B 48; On associationism, A 22; On Fourierism, B 46.

Greene, Walter L., D 84.

Greer, Louise, D 39.

Griscomb, Stewart, D 40.

"Guest, A": Description of Brook Farm, B 49.

Guiney, Louise Imogen, F 4.

Haney, John Louis, D 41.

Haraszti, Zoltán: The Idyll of Brook Farm, D 40, D 42, D 43, D 74, G 2, G 5–G 8, G 10, G 12–G 15, G 17, G 18, G 20–G 22, G 24, G 26, G 28, G 29.

Harbinger, A 121, A 131, A 132, C 2, D 82, G 19, G 25, G 27, G 31, G 50; Articles in, A 2, A 3, A 6, A 41, A 102, A 104, B 17, D 52, D 74, E 1, E 2, E 17; Dana on, G 48; Dial [Boston] and, E 3; J.S. Dwight and, A 45; Emerson on, B 29; History of, E 1, E 4, E 5, E 7, E 13, E 14; Literary reviews in, E 4, E 11; On drama, D 33;
On French literature, E 9; On French Revolution, E 6; On German literature, E 18; On music, E 12; On G. Sand, E 8, E 10, E 15; On E. Sue, E 10, E 15; Phalanx and, C 22; Poe and, C 19, C 24; Ripley and, E 6; Ripley on, E 16, E 17; Subscriptions to, E 2, G 14, G 19, G 29, G 209, G 218; Whittier on, A 39, C 27.

Harding, Walter, D 64, D 74.

Harper's New Monthly Magazine, A 26–A 29, A 31, A 109, B 20, B 39, F 4.

Harper's Weekly Magazine, A 22.

Harris, Lilian I., D 44, D 45.

Hart, A. Bloomer: Description of Brook Farm, B 50.

Harvard Graduate's Magazine, A 22.

Harvard University, A 115.

Haverstick, Iola, D 26.

Hawthorne, Julian, A 70, A 71.

Hawthorne, Louisa: Letters to, D 74.

Hawthorne, Manning, A 72, D 74.

Hawthorne, Nathaniel, A 18, A 62, A 64, A 65, A 68, A 71, A 73, A 75, A 78–A 80, A 83, A 84, B 30, D 30, D 52; American Notebooks, A 50, A 51, D 26, D 74; The Blithedale Romance, A 52, A 55–A 60, A 63, A 66, A 69, A 74, A 81, A 85, A 136, B 41, D 26, D 49, D 74; Compared with Emerson, A 66, A 76; Compared with Melville, A 57; Curtis on, A 25, A 26; Dana and, A 77; Description of, A 61, A 134, A 135, G 6; "Hall of Fantasy," A 53; Journals by: see American Notebooks; Letters by, A 54, A 70, A 72, A 77, D 74; Ripley and, A 77; Ripley on,

113

B 55; Transcendentalism and, A 67, A 76, A 80.

Hawthorne, Sophia Peabody. See Sophia Peabody.

Haynes, George H., A 22.

Hecker, Isaac T., A 86–A 90, B 8, D 76; Curtis on, A 25, A 88; Description of, A 134, A 135; Journals by, A 88–A 90; Letters by, A 88–A 90, D 26, D 74; Letters to, D 26.

Hecker, John: Letters by, B 8, G 228.

Helmcke, Hans, A 74.

Henry E. Huntington Library, D 74.

Herald Tribune Book Review [New York], D 64.

Herrnstadt, Richard L., B 3.

Higginson, Mary Thacher, B 53, B 54.

Higginson, Thomas Wentworth, A 22, D 74; Description of Brook Farm, B 54; Journals by, B 54; Letters by, B 53; On Dana, B 53; On Fuller, B 41; Recollections of Brook Farm, B 51, B 52.

Hilen, Andrew, C 17.

Hillard, George, A 77.

Hillquit, Morris, D 46.

Hislop, Codman, D 15.

Historian, D 23.

Hochfield, George, D 47.

Holbrook, Josiah, D 91.

Holbrook, Stewart H., F 5.

Holden, Vincent F., A 89, A 90.

Holloway, Mark, D 48.

Holmes, Oliver Wendell, A 81.

Home, Washington, Community, F 5.

Hosmer, James Kendall: Recollections of Brook Farm, B 55.

Hosum, George H.: Letters by, G 39.

Howe, Julia Ward, A 4.

Howe, Leonard, and Co., A 114.

Howells, William Dean, A 22.

Hudspeth, Robert N., B 42.

Hughes, Riley, D 64.

Huidekoper, Harm Jan: Letters by, C 25.

Huntington, Arria S., B 56.

Huntington, Frederic Dan; Description of Brook Farm, B 56.

Illustrations: Articles, A 17, A 71, D 10, D 19, D 25, D 27, D 32, D 42, D 44, D 45, D 56, D 60, D 78, D 84; Books, A 16, A 48, A 63, A 133, D 12, D 20, D 43, D 52, D 61.

Independent, A 48, A 133.

Infant School Society, D 91.

Inland Printer, D 44.

Isely, Jeter A., A 116.

Isely, Lisette Riggs, A 116, A 119.

Italian-language studies, D 96.

James, Henry, A 73.

James, Myrle, A 117.

Johns Hopkins University Studies in Historical and Political Science, A 24.

Johnson, Jane Maloney, D 49.

Johnson, Judith Kennedy, A 98.

Johnson, Rossiter, A 133.

Jones, Howard Mumford, E 8.

Jones, John Dillon, D 50.

Jordan, John W., C 16.

"Journal B. Brook Farm," G 204.

Journal of the American Musico-
  logical Society, E 12.
Journal of the History of Ideas,
  D 22.
Joyaux, Georges Jules, E 9,
  E 10.

Kansas State Historical Society,
  A 15, G 33–G 51.
Kaufman, Marjorie Ruth, E 11.
Kay, James: Letters by, B 57,
  G 21, G 26, G 215–G 217;
  Letters to, G 13.
Kelley, Edythe Loretto, D 51.
Kinoy, Arthur. See Channing
  Edwards.
Kirby, Georgiana Bruce: Letters
  by, D 82, G 19; Description
  of Brook Farm, A 91–A 96;
  Years of Experience, A 96,
  D 74, D 76.
Kirkus, D 64.
Knortz, Karl, B 43.
Kromer, Helen, D 52.

Lamp, D 45.
Lane, Charles, A 22, D 74;
  Description of, A 93, G 39;
  Description of Brook Farm,
  B 58, B 59; Letters by, B 58.
Lang, Hans-Joachim, A 74.
Lathrop, George Parsons, A 75.
Lauderbaugh, Stanley J., D 53.
Leader [New York], A 105.
Legasse, Viola May, A 118.
Lennon, Florence Becker, A 32.
Letters, A 85.
Library Journal, D 64.
Lindell, Mildred Helene, D 54.
List, Christopher: Letters by,
  G 13.

Literary Digest, A 133.
Littell's Living Age, A 105.
Longfellow, Henry Wadsworth:
  Letters by, C 17; On Ripley,
  C 17.
Longfellow, Samuel: Letters by,
  G 12.
Lowell, James Russell: Letters
  to, A 46.
Lowens, Irving, E 12.
Lubbers, Klaus, A 74.

McAvoy, Thomas T., B 9.
Macdaniel, Fanny: Letters by,
  G 32.
McDonald, John Alfred, D 55.
McElderry, B.R., Jr., A 76.
McGill University Magazine, D 36.
McGinley, A.A., D 56.
Mack, David, A 72.
Mack, Mrs. David: Description of
  Brook Farm, C 14.
Mackintosh, Charles G., D 57.
MacNab, John E., D 58.
McSorley, Joseph, D 15.
Madden, Edward H., A 33.
Magazine of Books [Chicago
  Tribune], D 64.
Manuscripts, A 107.
Marsh, Fred T., D 15.
Marsh, James: Letters by, C 18,
  C 26; Letters to, A 110.
Massachusetts Historical Society,
  A 48, G 52–G 206.
Master of Arts theses, A 32,
  A 56, A 58, A 60, A 67, A 80,
  A 81, A 84, A 117, A 118,
  A 126, B 46, D 29, D 34, D 50,
  D 51, D 53–D 55, D 59, D 65,
  D 69, D 70, D 73, D 85, D 88,
  E 6, E 11, E 14.

Matle, John H., B 34.
Maynard, Theodore, B 10.
Melville, Herman: Compared with Hawthorne, A 57.
Menzi, Marjorie Jean, D 59.
Metzdorf, Robert F., A 77.
Michael, Cecelia Koretsky, B 46.
Middlebury College Library, D 74, G 207-G 225.
Midwest Quarterly, A 76.
Milne, Gordon, A 34.
Missionary, A 123.
Mitchell, Anna M., D 60.
Mitchell, Donald G., D 61.
Modern Language Notes, A 115.
Monthly Miscellany of Religion and Letters, A 106, B 1, D 74.
More Books, A 100, D 40, D 42, D 43.
Morris, Lloyd, A 78.
Moss, Sydney P., C 19.
Mott, Frank Luther, E 13.
Mullan, William, F 6.
Muncy, Raymond Lee, D 62.
Music at Brook Farm, A 27, A 29, A 43, A 100, D 74, E 12.
Myerson, Joel, A 97, B 42, C 20, D 32, D 63.

Nation, A 22, A 25, A 133, D 15, D 82.
National Anti-Slavery Standard, B 26.
National Era, C 27.
National Magazine, D 84.
Nelson, Truman: Passion by the Brook, D 64.
Nerber, John, D 64.

New Age, Concordium Gazette, and Temperance Advocate, B 58.
New England Farmer and Horticultural Register, C 1.
New England Galaxy, A 68.
New England Magazine, A 136, D 19.
New England Quarterly, A 72, A 83, A 97, B 32, D 9, D 15, D 33, D 91, E 15.
New Moral World, B 36, B 37.
New Republic, B 27, D 15, D 64.
New Statesman and Nation, A 79.
New-York Daily Tribune, A 7, B 6, B 62, C 8.
New-York Observer, C 8.
New York Times, A 135.
New York Times Book Review, A 48, D 15, D 26, D 64.
New-York Tribune, B 46, B 47.
New-York Weekly Tribune, A 103, B 62, C 2, C 11.
Newcomb, Charles King, A 98, D 76; Description of, A 48, A 92, A 93.
Nissenbaum, Stephen, D 65.
North American Phalanx, D 26.
Northampton Association, D 9.
Norton, Andrews, A 120.
Noyes, John Humphrey, B 19, D 66.
Nuntius Aulae, D 67.

Old and New, A 91, A 93-A 96.
Orvis, John, A 99, A 102, G 182; Description of, A 48; Letters by, G 29, G 218-G 222.
Orvis, Marianne Dwight. See Marianne Dwight.
Osgood, Samuel: Letters by, G 5, G 14.

Ossoli, Sarah Margaret Fuller. See Sarah Margaret Fuller.

Ostinelli, Frances, A 100.

Outlook, F 2.

Overland Monthly, A 49, A 92, A 96.

Parker, Theodore: Compared with Curtis, A 33; Compared with Ripley, A 120; Description of, A 93; Letters to, G 214; Transcendentalism and, A 33.

Parsons, Anna Q.T.: Letters by, G 63, G 80, G 85–G 88, G 101, G 112, G 119–G 121, G 123, G 124, G 133, G 136, G 140, G 148, G 153, G 165, G 174, G 187, G 198–G 200, G 224; Letters to, A 48, G 52–G 57, G 59, G 60, G 62, G 66, G 70, G 75, G 77, G 82, G 90, G 92–G 94, G 96, G 99, G 103, G 106, G 113, G 114, G 122, G 128, G 131, G 135, G 141–G 144, G 146, G 147, G 149–G 152, G 154, G 158, G 160, G 167, G 169–G 173, G 175, G 176, G 179, G 182–G 186, G 188–G 193, G 195–G 197.

Pax, Joseph M., D 67.

Peabody, Elizabeth Palmer, B 60–B 62, C 21, D 47, D 74; Letters by, G 4, G 6, G 8.

Peabody, Sophia, A 76; Letters by, A 70; Letters to, A 54, A 70, D 74.

Personalist, A 33, A 57.

Pestalozzian Society, D 91.

Phalanstery, A 6, A 22, A 104, A 131, A 132, C 2, D 52, D 95, G 24, G 211, G 223, G 224. See also Brook Farm, Buildings and Land; Brook Farm, Fire at.

Phalanx, C 22; Articles in, A 5, A 35, A 37, B 49, B 50, C 3–C 7, C 10, C 22, D 74, E 16; Harbinger and, C 22.

Ph.D. dissertations, A 45, A 59, A 119, A 121, D 5, D 37, D 49, E 4, E 9.

Phillips, Paul, A 22.

Philological Quarterly, B 57.

Pickard, John B., C 27.

Pierce, Edward L., C 23.

Pioneer, A 53.

Pochmann, Henry A., A 120.

Pocumtuck Valley Memorial Association Proceedings, A 131.

Poe, Edgar Allan: Harbinger and, C 19, C 24.

Powell, Janette C., E 14.

Pratt, Frederick: Recollections of Brook Farm, A 97.

Present, B 18.

Printing Group, G 202.

Pritchett, V.S., A 79.

Proceedings of the Unitarian Historical Society, A 116, D 6, D 58.

Purchase Street Church, A 111, G 1.

Puritanism, D 37.

Putnam, Hannah S., D 68.

R., W.K., D 15.

Rabinovitz, Albert L., E 15.

Raymond, Henrietta Dana, A 126.

Reed, Amy L., A 48.

Reilly, Reverend Francis A., D 69.

Religion at Brook Farm, A 36, D 34, D 74. See also Catholicism, Unitarianism.

Rhode Island History, D 24.

Riasanovsky, Nicholas V., C 15.

Riggs, Lisette. See Lisette Riggs Isely.

117

Ripley, George, A 8, A 11,
A 102–A 106, A 108, A 111–
A 113, A 119, A 121, B 65,
C 13, C 20, C 21, D 26, D 52,
D 73, D 74, D 95, G 2, G 5,
G 8, G 23, G 51; Brownson
and, B 8, G 229; Carlyle on,
C 12; Compared with Alcott,
D 29; Compared with Curtis,
A 33; Compared with Emerson,
D 29; Compared with Parker,
A 120; Description of, A 48,
A 94, A 127, A 136, C 20;
Education and, A 117; Emerson
on, B 22; Fourierism and,
D 21; German philosophy and,
A 120; Harbinger and, A 121,
E 6, E 11, E 16, E 17; Haw-
thorne and, A 77; Journals
by, A 115; Letters by, A 22,
A 107, A 109, A 110, B 8,
C 18, D 47, G 1, G 3, G 24,
G 41, G 225, G 226, G 229;
Letters to, D 47, G 23;
Library of, A 114; Longfellow
on, C 17; On Fourier, A 5; On
Hawthorne, B 55; Poem on
Brook Farm, A 101; Transcen-
dentalism and, A 33, A 106,
A 108, A 116–A 118, A 120;
Unitarianism and, A 120;
Utopian socialism and, A 108;
Utopianism and, A 118.

Ripley, Hannah: Letters to,
G 34, G 37, G 40, G 46–G 51.

Ripley, Sophia Willard Dana,
A 119, A 122–A 126, G 51;
Description of, A 40, A 48,
A 125–A 127; Letters by,
A 119, A 126, G 2, G 7, G 22.

Rodgers, Ada S., D 70.

Ross, Charles Emmett, A 80.

Roxbury, Massachusetts. Joint
Special Committee, D 71,
D 72.

Rugoff, Milton, D 64.

Rusk, Ralph L., B 25.

Russell, Amelia E.: Recollections of Brook Farm, A 127,
A 128, D 74.

Russell, Wing: Letters by, G 34.

Ryll, Charlyn Tye, D 73.

S., W.G.H., A 99.

Salisbury, Annie M.: Recollections of Brook Farm, A 129,
A 130.

Sams, Henry W.: Autobiography of
Brook Farm, D 74, D 75, G 213,
G 219, G 220, G 225.

Sanborn, F.B., A 4, D 63, D 76,
D 82.

Sand, George: Harbinger and,
E 8, E 10, E 15.

Saturday Review of Literature,
D 14, D 15.

Saxton, S. Willard: Recollections
of Brook Farm, A 119, A 131,
A 132.

Sceery, Edwin James, D 77.

Schlesinger, Arthur M., Jr.,
B 11.

Schlueter, Paul, D 26.

Schmidt-v. Bardeleben, Renate,
A 74.

Scholastic, D 10.

School and Society, D 26, D 92.

Schultz, Arthur R., A 120.

Scott, Leonora Cranch, B 21.

Sears, John Van Der Zee: My
Friends at Brook Farm, A 133,
D 74.

Sedgwick, Ora Gannett: Recollections of Brook Farm, A 18,
A 134, A 135, D 74.

Shakers, D 80.

Sharp, Nancy Weatherly, D 26.

Shepard, Odell, B 2, D 15.

Sherwood, M.E.W.: Recollections
of Brook Farm, B 63.

Shuman, R. Baird, A 46.

Simpson, Claude M., A 51.
Skeneatales Community, B 14.
Sketch [England], A 9.
Slater, Joseph, B 22.
Smart, George K., D 78.
Snell, Joseph W., A 15.
Snider, Denton J., B 35.
Socialism, A 16, D 22, D 46, D 58, D 68, G 51; W.H. Channing and, D 66; Greeley on, B 47; Hawthorne on, A 55.
Southeran, Charles, B 47.
Southwest Review, C 20.
Spencer, Benjamin T., D 79.
Spring, Marcus, B 19, G 23; Letters by, G 27.
Springfield Republican, D 15, D 76, D 82.
Stanton, Elizabeth Cady: Recollections of Brook Farm, B 64.
Star [New York], A 1.
Stearns, Frank Preston, B 65.
Stearns, George Luther, B 65.
Stebbins, Giles B.: Recollections of Brook Farm, B 66.
Stern, Madeleine B., B 44.
Stewart, Randall, A 50, A 51.
Stillman, Clara Gruening, D 15.
Stocks [Brook Farm's], G 23, G 206.
Stoddard, Henry Luther, B 48.
Stoehr, Taylor, D 80.
Studies in the American Renaissance, B 42, D 32.
Sturgis, James: Recollections of Brook Farm, A 8.
Sue, Eugène: Harbinger and, E 10, E 15.
Sumner, Arthur: Recollections of Brook Farm, A 136, D 74.

Sumner, Charles: Letters by, C 23.
Sumner, Horace, C 23.
Sveino, Per, B 12.
Swedenborgianism, D 66.
Swift, Lindsay: Brook Farm, A 48, D 26, D 74, D 81, D 82.

T., C.B., D 83.
Tarbell, Arthur W., D 84.
Technology Review, D 27.
This World [San Francisco Chronicle], D 26.
Thomas, J. Wesley, A 47.
Thoreau, Henry David, D 76; Letters to, D 74.
Thurman, Kelly, A 81.
Tiffany, Francis, C 25.
Tiffany, Nina Moore, C 25.
Tileston, Mary Wilder, C 14.
Times Literary Supplement, A 48, D 15.
Titus, Eunice E., D 85.
Transcendental Club, G 4.
Transcendentalism, A 25, B 7, B 62, C 12, D 23, D 29, D 32, D 33, D 35, D 37, D 53, D 59, D 70, D 77, D 80, D 88, D 90, D 96; Curtis and, A 33; Fourierism and, D 22, D 32; Hawthorne and, A 67, A 76, A 80; Music and, E 12; Parker and, A 33; Ripley and, A 33, A 106, A 108, A 116–A 118, A 120.
Traubel, Horace, D 82.
Travel, D 78.
Trent, William P., D 86.
Turner, Arlin, A 82, A 83.
Turrell, Carolyn, A 84.
Tweedy, Edward: Letters by, G 25.
Tyler, Alice Felt, D 87.

Undergraduate honors theses, D 68.

Unitarianism, D 6, D 49, D 58, D 65; Ripley and, A 120.

United States Magazine and Democratic Review, B 6, B 8, C 15.

University of California Publications in Modern Philology, D 35.

University of Chicago, D 74.

University of Kansas City Review, A 55.

University of Michigan: Dana's address at, A 38.

University of Notre Dame Library, B 9, G 226–G 231.

University of Texas Studies in English, A 82.

Utopian socialism, D 24, D 55; Hawthorne and, A 72; Ripley and, A 108.

Utopianism, D 41, D 53; Ripley and, A 118.

Vogel, Stanley M., E 18.

Wallster, Jeanne A., D 88.

Ward, William Smith, A 85.

Waters, Edwin F.: Recollections of Brook Farm, A 19.

Webber, Everett, D 89, G 213.

Wells, Roland Vale, C 18, C 26.

Wendell, Barrett, D 90.

Whalen, Doran, B 13.

Whittier, John Greenleaf: Letters by, C 27; On Harbinger, A 39, C 27.

Wilkenson, Dr., G 25.

Wilson, Howard Aaron, A 121.

Wilson, John B., D 91, D 92.

Wilson, James Harrison, A 38.

Wilson, Rufus Rockwell, D 93.

Winsor, Justin, A 11.

Wisconsin Library Bulletin, D 15.

Wolfe, Theodore F., D 94.

Women's rights, D 59.

Worthley, Evans A., D 95.

Zenobia: Fuller as, A 81, B 41. See also Nathaniel Hawthorne, The Blithedale Romance.

Zolla, Elémire, D 96.